Wild
Flowers
of
Westerdale

With best wishes
and happy memories

Carol

First published by the
North Yorkshire Moors Association, 2019

A Catalogue in Publication record for this book is available from the British Library

ISBN 978-0-9565779-6-2

All photographs © Carol Wilson unless otherwise indicated

Design and typeset by Basement Press (www.basementpress.com)

Printed and bound in the UK by Toad Design Group
(www.toaddiaries.co.uk – www.toadbookbinders.co.uk)

This book is produced using paper that is grown in managed sustainable forests. The logging and
manufacturing processes conform to the environmental regulations of the country of origin.

Wild Flowers of Westerdale

Carol M Wilson

For Rebecca and Jonathan with love

And in memory of Francesca Garforth and Emma Beeforth, late of Westerdale.
If there are any errors in my Latin, Francesca will find a way
to let me know and Emma will simply say 'very well'.

Contents

Acknowledgements

ALTHOUGH it is my name that appears on the front cover of this book I am very much aware that none of it would have happened without the help of many people.

Firstly, I must thank my husband, Nigel, for his unfailing encouragement and support throughout the collecting of material, writing and publication of this book. He has my undying gratitude for making this possible.

Nor would this book have happened without the help and contribution of Vincent Jones, vice-county recorder for North East Yorkshire (vc 62) for the Botanical Society of Britain and Ireland. Vince has given unstintingly of his time to help with the recording of the plants around the dale. I am especially thankful for his help in identifying the roses, dandelions, brambles, willows and the solitary hawkweed. I am also very grateful to him for proofreading the text. Thanks to Albert Elliot too for reading the final proof. Thanks must also go to Pauline Popely for the introduction to Tom Higginbottom, plant gall recorder for the Yorkshire Naturalists' Union, who proofread the information on the galls and corrected my mistakes. I am also very grateful to Joyce Scott for identifying the lichens. Any remaining errors, however, are my own.

Thanks too to Kevin Walker who kindly gave me access to the BSBI records for Westerdale to enable me to use them as a check list against my own. I am also grateful for the interest, help and support from Nan Sykes. Nan has very kindly allowed me to use some of her photographs when I wasn't able to find suitable specimens; these are duly credited where appropriate. Thank you to Adrian Leaman for facilitating access to these. Thanks too to David Barlow for identifying the bracket fungi and for the use of some of his photographs of several plant species; these are also duly credited where appropriate.

Thanks must go to Pascal Thivillon for typesetting and image correction and to Nicola Chalton for proofreading the final draft. Their expertise has made an invaluable contribution to this book. I must also thank Claire Ford who gave me some valuable lessons in managing an SLR camera and for advice on taking microscope photographs. And of course to the North Yorkshire Moors Association for agreeing to publish the book. I must also give special thanks to NYMA for granting me a share in their President's Award for 2018, towards the costs of publication, for which I am very grateful.

Many thanks to my Westerdale neighbours who have pointed out plants to me. I am particularly indebted to Colin Grice, who knows the dale so well, who provided information about the elms and conifers and has often pointed me in the direction of a specimen I have missed. Colin also let me know where his cattle were so that I could safely walk his fields and even waited to move them from one field to another as long as I left a ribbon to say I was in a particular place; so glad not to get trampled.

Ribbonicus botanicus

I am grateful to the members of the North East Yorkshire Botany Group who have taken part in botany walks at Westerdale to help with identification and recording, in particular the sharp-eyed Wendy English. I must also thank all of those friends and family members who have been willing to accompany me on walks around Westerdale, especially to some of the more remote parts of the dale. In particular – Elaine Wisdom, Pam Shepherd, Ruth Brown, Roma Haigh, Hilary Harris, Lynne Bell, Joan Turnbull, Sharon Artley, Margaret Marsland (thanks for the loan of the wellies, Margaret!), Ashley and Jonny Benton (thanks for help with the rose gall) and Jonathan, Nicky, Beatrice and Aubrey Bennett. Your companionship has always been appreciated and those extra pairs of eyes have spotted specimens I might have missed.

Last but by no means least, I must thank my children, to whom this book is dedicated. Without them I may never have embarked on a botanical foray at all. When they were small and we were out for walks they would point to some flower or other and say 'Mummy what's that?' and then find something else and ask 'Oh, Mummy, what's this one?' I felt that I should be able to answer them but found that I couldn't. Living in Norfolk then, we joined the Norfolk Wildlife Trust and I spent weekends hanging on the coat tails of Richard Hobbs, the Trust's director at that time, learning the names of the plants we were likely to encounter on country walks. Thus began an absorbing hobby that has whiled away walks and many a country holiday and given endless pleasure. My heartfelt thanks and love to you both.

Carol Wilson
Westerdale 2019

Introduction

THE WILD plants included in this book are those found within the whole of Westerdale. The southern limit is the parish boundary, which includes Esklets; its northern limit is Baysdale Beck, although I have included plants on the beck's northern banks as part of this area is an SSSI and includes species of particular interest. Westerdaleside is its eastern edge, while the boundary to the west takes in Hograh Moor but does not include Baysdale. In other words, this is an area that could be covered by walking out from Westerdale village.

As soon as I moved to Westerdale in 2004, just for my own interest, I began to record the wild flowers that I found along the lanes and on the moorland. I then became aware that others might be interested in what they found when walking around this lovely dale and so I decided to record more seriously and to improve my own identification skills. This more serious recording has taken place since 2015 so that all seasons have been fully covered.

While there are several very good wild flower books on moorland flowers there is not a book on one specific dale. In view of the changes to our flora in recent years, due to the effects of climate change and the use of herbicides, it seemed appropriate to record, as it were, a snapshot in time of all the wild plants found in one relatively small area. To that end this modest volume does contain a record of all of the vascular plants, rather than just the wild flowers, and I have also included, for interest, some of the lichens and fungi found along the way.

The usual convention in a book such as this is for plants to be listed in botanical order. This means beginning with the simplest flowers of all, the poppy and buttercup families, (*Papaveraceae* and *Ranunculaceae)*, through to the more complex such as the orchid family (*Orchidaceae*). This assumes, however, a knowledge of features of plant families. While aiming for botanical accuracy, this book is intended for the general reader so a decision was made to compile most of the book in colour order so that anyone walking in Westerdale can look for 'a little blue job' (or any other colour) they might find when out walking.

Inevitably this poses problems of its own as one person's pink is another's purple and some people would call them all red! To avoid too much confusion the red, pink and purple flowers have been grouped together. Likewise, the differences between white and yellow become blurred at the edges so, inevitably, there have had to be some compromises and the one truly orange species has been included at the end of the section on yellow flowers. However, within each of the colour bands, the plants have still been listed within their families, in botanical order, and their family grouping is included within the text. A brief summary of family features can be found at the beginning of the book.

While all of the plants included here have been described, albeit briefly, a few are not illustrated but a similar species will be and the differences are noted. Several plants, especially rushes, sedges and grasses, have identification features that need to be looked for with the aid of a hand lens. A x10 hand lens is recommended for identification in the field. This level of magnification is easier to manage than anything higher and is enough to open up a whole new and fascinating world. Where

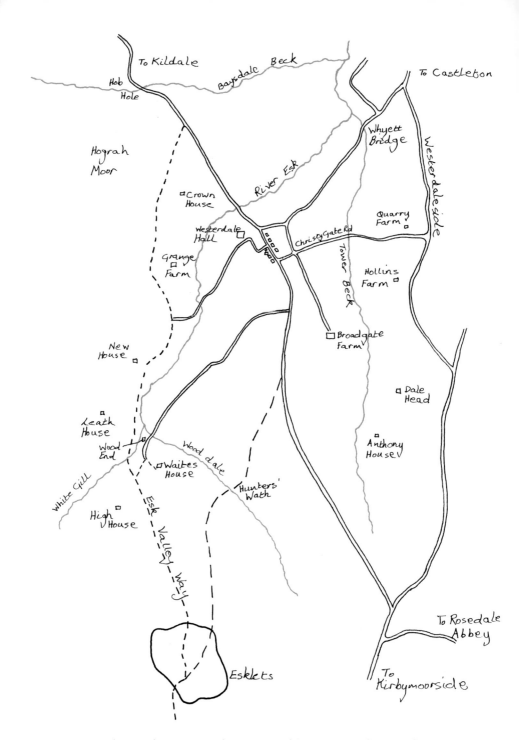

For location please see OS Landranger map 94 sheet NZ or OS Explorer Map sheet OL26.

plants are not illustrated, readers are directed to the reference section at the back of the book and are encouraged to use the recommended identification guides.

As I am particularly interested in the uses of plants in medieval times, especially their medicinal uses, I have included some of these details where relevant. However, readers should be wary of experimenting with any plant material, even if it has proven healing properties. It is always best to use commercially prepared treatments.

Botany is, in many ways, a language; there are specific terms for the different parts of plants. It has been unavoidable to include some of these terms. To aid understanding, a detailed glossary has been provided. In order to minimise text, abbreviations have been used in some cases. A list of these and their meanings can be found at the beginning of the book. Important identification features, especially those that distinguish one species from a similar one, are printed in *italics*. Similarly, where plants are known to be poisonous these are marked as such within the text.

For the technically minded:

Some of my earlier photographs were taken with a Fujifilm compact Finepix camera. This was usually used on automatic on a point-and-shoot basis, sometimes using its macro facility. Later images were taken with a Nikon 3300 SLR camera. These too were sometimes taken on automatic and/or using its macro facility but some were also taken using a short focal length or a fast shutter speed to accommodate flowers moving in the wind. The microscope images, presented in circles, were taken with a Nikon Coolpix P5100 automatic compact camera attached, via an adapter, to a Brunel stereo-microscope MX3. These images are x10, x20 or x30.

I would like to point out that when you are in the river in your wellies at eight in the morning, crouching down but trying to keep your bum dry, while managing a camera, attempting to photograph a specimen that is less than a centimetre in diameter and moving in a stiff breeze, these are far from studio conditions; I have done my best. Apologies for those images that are less than super sharp but I hope that they will all enable identification. Where I have not had clear photographs I have made line drawings of some species.

Please be aware that it is **illegal** to uproot any wild plant without the land owner's permission; in this case usually the North York Moors National Park or the estate owner. I have been told by Emma Skidmore and Valerie Watson, both of whom attended Westerdale School several decades ago, that each summer the children were encouraged to pick as many different varieties of wild flowers as they could find. There was a prize for the child finding the most, which Emma won one year. Such behaviour could not be permitted today. Where common plants are concerned no-one is going to mind a single specimen being picked – rather than uprooted. However, the days of gathering arms full of wild flowers are long gone. In the case of rarer species and especially orchids these should *never* be picked. Please take the book to the plants rather than the plants to the book to be able to identify them. As a general rule, as with all areas of the countryside, leave only footprints and take only photographs. Happy wild flower hunting.

Carol Wilson
Westerdale 2019

Abbreviations

agg	Aggregate	**sp**	Species (pl spp)
aka	Also known as	**ssp**	Subspecies –a division within a species
Bg 2014	Broadgate Farm, the site where wild flower seeds were sown in 2014	**SSSI**	Site of Special Scientific Interest
BSBI	Botanical Society of Britain and Ireland	**vc**	Vice-county. Since 1852, for the purposes of botanical identification and the recording of species, the whole of the UK has been divided into vice-counties. Westerdale lies in vc62. Each vc has a designated recorder of species.
c	*Circa*, Latin for about		
cf	*Conferre*, Latin for compare		
qv	*Quod vide*, Latin for which see (directing you to another piece in the book for more information)	**x**	Denotes a hybrid between two or more species.
pl	Plural		
sing	Singular		

Plant families

The following plant families are represented in Westerdale. These details give a brief outline of the main characteristics of each family in order to aid identification. The families are listed in botanical order. Except for the single liverwort and five lichens, which are included for interest, all of the entries here are *vascular* plants. Vascular plants - aka tracheophytes - have conducting tissue, called xylem and phloem, which behaves in a similar way to the veins in animals. Vascular tissue conducts water and mineral salts as well as providing physical support to the plant. Vascular plants include the **pteridophytes, gymnosperms** and **angiosperms**.

PTERIDOPHYTES – these are the simplest of the vascular plants, comprising ferns, horsetails and clubmosses. They first appeared on earth millions of years ago. As there are no clubmosses found in Westerdale these will not be described here. Pteridophytes are non-flowering plants growing from rhizomes and reproducing by spores.

Adder's tongue family *Ophioglossaceae*
A eusporangiate fern, that is a fern having the sporangia (spore producing organs) developing from several cells rather than a single cell. Unmistakable with a single sterile leaf-like blade and a single fertile spike. Represented in Westerdale by a solitary Adder's tongue.

Horsetail family *Equisetaceae*
Herbaceous perennials with long rhizomes. Aerial stems are jointed, often unbranched or with branches in whorls around the stem. A characteristic feature of horsetails is the whorl of very narrow leaves forming a fused sheath around the stems. Cones are borne on top of fertile stems usually appearing earlier than

vegetative stems. Not to be confused with mare's-tails, *Hippuris* sp, family *Hippuridaceae*, not found in Westerdale.

FERN FAMILIES:

The leaves of ferns are known as *fronds* with a mid-rib called a *rachis*. Fronds are usually spirally coiled, like a fiddle head, when young. They are often divided; pinnate, bipinnate or tripinnate. Reproduction is by spores held in sori (sing. sorus) on underside of fronds. Shape and position of sori are often keys to identification. Sori are sometimes covered with a structure known as the indusium.

The ferns found in Westerdale fall into several discrete families:

Bracken family *Dennstaedtiaceae*
Formerly *Hypolepidaceae*
Fern with extensive rhizomes, often deep underground. Stipe and rachis very strong. Fronds borne singly, without scales. Sori along margins of pinnae.

Spleenwort family *Aspleniaceae*
Rhizomes short, with scales. Fronds in tufts, usually with scales on the underside. Sori rectangular, sometimes long and linear. Family represented in Westerdale by hart's tongue (*Asplenium scolopendrium*).

Marsh fern family *Thelypteridaceae*

Rhizomes long and slender or short and thick, usually with scales. Fronds borne singly or in dense tufts with sparse scales, 2x pinnate. Sori in a row on underside of pinnule usually close to margin. Indusium absent or soon withering. Family represented in Westerdale by lemon-scented fern (*Oreopteris limbosperma*).

Lady fern family *Woodsiaceae*

Formerly *Arythriaceae*. Rhizomes of varying length, with scales. Fronds usually in tufts, sometimes singly, 1-4x pinnate. Sori variable, with or without indusia. Family represented in Westerdale by lady fern (*Athyrium filix-femina*).

Hard fern family *Blechnaceae*

Rhizomes of varying lengths, scaly. Fronds leathery, borne in tufts, sparsely scaly. Family represented in Westerdale by hard fern (*Blechnum spicant*).

Buckler fern family *Dryopteridaceae*

Rhizomes short and densely scaly. Fronds with scales, in tufts, spirally coiled when young, 1-3x pinnate. Sori round, covered by indusia. Three members of this family found in Westerdale.

GYMNOSPERMS – non-flowering plants

aka conifers; trees or shrubs with simple, usually evergreen, leaves. Male sporangia held within male cones; female sporangia borne in naked ovules either singly or held in female cones.

Pine family *Pinaceae*

Evergreen, resin-producing trees. Leaves needle-like, borne in spirals, on long shoots or in clusters. Monoecious, female cones with spirally arranged cone scales. Seeds winged, detaching at maturity. Distinguished from other coniferous trees by the spirally-borne very narrow leaves and the distinct bracts below each cone scale.

Yew family *Taxaceae*

Evergreen trees or shrubs. Leaves linear, borne spirally. Distinguished from other conifers by being non-resinous. Usually dioecious, male and female cones very small. Female develops into a succulent aril.

Juniper family *Cupressaceae*

Formerly *Taxodiaceae*. Evergreen, resin-producing trees or shrubs. Vegetative buds without bud scales. Leaves opposite, whorled or borne in spirals; needle-like or scale-like. Monoecious or dioecious; female cones with woody or succulent scales. Distinguished from the pine family (*Pinaceae*) by lack of bud scales and the indistinct bracts fused to the cone scales.

PRE-DICOTS – Primitive angiosperms

Bay family *Lauraceae*

Evergreen trees or shrubs. Leaves aromatic, entire, alternate and without stipules. Dioecious with flowers solitary or in small clusters in leaf axils. Male flowers with 8-12 stamens, female flowers with 2-4 staminodes and a single-celled ovary. Fruit a single-seeded black berry.

DICOTYLEDONS – flowering plants with

two seed leaves following germination.

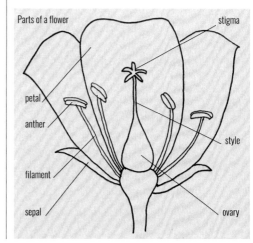

Parts of a flower

stigma

petal

anther

style

filament

sepal

ovary

Poppy family *Papaveraceae*

Herbaceous annuals or perennials. Sepals usually falling as soon as flowers open. Petals usually large and brightly coloured, crumpled on opening. Fruit an achene or capsule. Includes poppies and fumitories; DNA evidence has shown that they are more closely related than appears.

Buttercup family *Ranunculaceae*

Herbaceous plants, sometimes woody climbers. Considered primitive in evolutionary terms. Flowers with many stamens and five petals or petal-like sepals, sometimes referred to as tepals. Fruits many achenes. Includes buttercups, crowfoots, columbine and wood anemone.

Gooseberry family *Grossulariaceae*

Deciduous shrubs; leaves alternate without stipules. Flowers solitary or in racemes, bisexual or dioecious. Distinguished by 5 petals shorter than sepals. Fruit a berry.

Saxifrage family *Saxifragaceae*

Annual or perennial herbs not usually woody at the base. Flowers with 3 styles and 4 or 5 petals. Leaves either alternate along the stem or in a basal rosette. Fruit a capsule.

Stonecrop family *Crassulaceae*

Annual or perennial, hairless herbs with succulent leaves. Flowers star-like with 5 petals. Low growing, often colonising walls or path edges.

Pea family *Fabaceae*

Formerly *Leguminaceae*. Variable family including annual and perennial herbs, shrubs and trees. Leaves alternate, trefoil or pinnate, sometimes with tendrils. Characterised by zygomorphic flowers with 5 irregular petals, an upper standard, two narrow wings at each side and two lower petals joined to form the keel, each with 10 stamens. Fruit a pod, hence leguminous. All legumes have nodes along their roots which hold rhizobia that are able to fix nitrogen from the air in such a way as to make it useable by the plants, which makes *Fabaceae* of considerable economic and ecological importance. This family includes broom and gorse, clovers and vetches as well as peas.

Milkwort family *Polygalaceae*

Low growing, slender, hairless perennials. Leaves oval, in pairs. Flowers somewhat flattened with 5 sepals, 3 of which are small and green, 2 of which are larger and coloured; these enclose 3 pale petals. Only one species represents this family in Westerdale.

Rose family *Rosaceae*

A large plant family including many trees and shrubs as well as annual or perennial herbs. Leaves usually compound with stipules, growing alternately along the stem. Flowers variable with 5 sepals and 5 petals and many yellow stamens. Includes cherry, plum, hawthorn and blackberry, lady's mantle and meadowsweet as well as roses. Some roses have miniscule perfume glands on upper surface of their leaves or petals that exude the chemical geraniol, combined with other substances, which makes them aromatic.

Elm family *Ulmaceae*

Unmistakable deciduous trees with simple leaves, asymmetrical at the base, with stipules when young. Flowers bisexual, inconspicuous, in small clusters, produced before leaves. Fruits with 2 extending wings.

Nettle family *Urticaceae*

Annual or perennial herbaceous plants. Flowers inconspicuous, dioecious. Fruit an achene.

Beech family *Fagaceae*

Deciduous or evergreen trees, leaves simple, with stipules when young. Flowers monoecious, inconspicuous; male a catkin, female with 3-6-celled ovary. Fruit a nut surrounded by a cupule.

Birch family *Betulaceae*

Deciduous trees or shrubs with simple leaves with stipules when young. Flowers monoecious. Male flowers pendant catkins, female flowers usually erect catkins with 2 styles and 2-celled ovary. Fruit a nut, winged or not.

Wood-sorrel family *Oxalidaceae*

Herbaceous perennials with bulbils. Leaves trifoliate. Flowers with delicate-looking bowed heads, 5 petals. Two species represent this family in Westerdale.

Spurge family *Euphorbaceae*

Annual or perennial herbs. Stems with bitter latex. Leaves usually alternate, oval. Flowers tiny without true sepals or petals but with yellowish, sepal-like bracts. Includes dog's mercury as well as the spurges.

Willow family *Salicaceae*

Deciduous, dioecious catkin-bearing trees or shrubs with simple flowers and plumed seeds borne in a capsule. Includes osiers, poplars and aspen as well as all the familiar willows.

Violet family *Violaceae*

Annual or perennial herbs with leaves in a basal rosette. Solitary, zygomorphic flowers on longish stalks with 5 unequal sepals and 5 irregular petals, lowest one with a spur. In late summer some species produce inconspicuous structures known as cleistogamous flowers, which remain closed and self-pollinate. Includes the familiar pansies and violets.

Flax family *Linaceae*

Herbaceous annuals. Leaves opposite, undivided. Flowers with 5 petals. Includes flax, plants once grown in Westerdale for the production of linen, as well as fairy flax.

St John's wort family *Hypericaceae*

Hairless perennial herbs, leaves opposite and untoothed, without stipules or petioles and often with translucent glands. Flowers with 5 green sepals, 5 yellow petals and many stamens. Translucent leaf glands or black glands on margins of flower parts help to identify species, use lens to view.

Crane's-bill family *Geraniaceae*

Herbaceous annuals or perennials, most species very hairy. Flowers with 5 petals, variable in size but usually pink, mauve or blue. Distinctive fruits with 5 segments which curl upwards and end in a long 'beak': the crane's bill. Herb Robert is a member of the crane's-bill family.

Willowherb family *Onagraceae*

Herbaceous perennials. Leaves opposite, undivided. Stigmas either club- or cross-shaped; shape of stigma crucial for species identification. Flowers usually pink with 4 notched petals. Seeds, with long silky hairs, held in 4-sided pods that split on ripening.

Maple family *Sapindaceae*

Deciduous trees separated into three different genera two of which are represented in Westerdale by horse-chestnut (*Aesculus hippocastanum*) and sycamore (*Acer pseudoplatanus*). *Aesculus*: deciduous trees distinguished by their palmate, opposite leaves with long petioles. Flowers bisexual in long terminal panicle – the familiar 'candle'. *Acer*: deciduous trees with opposite, usually lobed leaves. Flowers terminal or in raceme-like panicle. Recognised by fruits in 2 parts each with 1 seed and a long wing.

Mallow family *Malvaceae*

Annual or perennial herbs. Leaves alternate along the stem, palmate or deeply cut. Flowers with a double row of sepals, sometimes fused at the base, and 5 notched, usually pink, petals. Fruit a disc-shaped nutlet.

Nasturtium family *Tropaeolaceae*

A family of fleshy vines or herbs with zygomorphic flowers having a nectary spur, eight stamens and ovaries with three compartments. This family consists of just one genus (*Tropaeolum*) with its 95 species all native to South America. Only *Tropaeolum speciosum* is found in Westerdale and that was originally planted.

Cabbage family *Brassicaceae*

Formerly *Cruciferae*. Herbaceous annuals or perennials. Flowers with 6 stamens, 4 sepals and 4 crosswise petals, hence sometimes referred to as crucifers; head elongating after flowering. Seeds held in a pod, sometimes with a short beak. Pods long and thin known as siliquae; broader pods known as siliculae. Includes shepherd's purse and lady's smock as well as rockets, mustards, radish and cabbage.

Dock family *Polygonaceae*

Herbaceous annuals or perennials with simple leaves. Recognised by stipules at base of leaves and characteristic papery sheath, known as an ochrea, at leaf-nodes. Flowers very small, usually red or brown with 6 petaloid sepals or tepals. Fruit a three-sided nut with one or three small warts (hand lens needed to view). Dead flowering stems persist through the winter. Often known as dockens in the north of England.

Sundew family *Droseraceae*

Insectivorous perennials with a basal rosette of leaves covered in red sticky hairs. Hairs curve inwards to trap insects on which the plant feeds. Flowers white with 5 petals on slender leafless stalks. Grows on wet boggy ground, occasionally found on sphagnum moss.

Pink family *Caryophyllaceae*

Herbaceous annuals or perennials, sometimes with woody lower stems. Stems swollen at the nodes, leaves in opposite pairs, untoothed and unstalked. Flower stalks repeatedly forked. Flowers with 4 or 5 sepals and 4 or 5 petals. Petals sometimes notched. Includes stitchworts, chickweeds, mouse-ears and campions as well as pinks.

Goosefoot family *Amaranthaceae*

This family now includes all of those formerly categorised as *Chenopodaceae*. Herbaceous annuals or perennials. Dull-coloured, plants with inconspicuous flowers having 5 sepals and no petals. Includes fat hen and orache.

Blinks family *Montiaceae*

Herbaceous annuals or perennials. Leaves usually basal, alternate or opposite. Flowers usually solitary with 2 sepals and 5 petals and 3-5 stamens. This family is represented in Westerdale by blinks and pink purslane.

Balsam family *Balsaminaceae*

Annual herbs. Leaves simple, alternate, opposite or in whorls of 3. Flower form unique with spurred lower sepals and 5 petals but appearing as 3 as 2 pairs fused. Only Himalayan balsam (*Impatiens glandulifera*) found in Westerdale and that is being eradicated.

Primrose family *Primulaceae*

Herbaceous annuals or perennials. Leaves without stipules, undivided in basal rosette. Sepals usually 5 with as many petals and stamens, petals fused at the base. Includes chickweed-wintergreen as well as yellow pimpernel and primrose.

Heath family *Ericaceae*

Usually evergreen, occasionally deciduous somewhat woody herbs that prefer acid soil. Referred to as sub-shrubs. Leaves small, often in whorls around stem. Flowers usually pink or purple, often bell-shaped. Fruit a capsule or berry. Includes bilberry and crowberry as well as the familiar heaths and heather.

Bedstraw family *Rubiaceae*

Annual or perennial herbs often climbing or scrambling. Leaves undivided and in whorls around the stem, leaf-like stipules. Flowers with very small or no sepals and 4 petals fused at the base. Fruit usually a nutlet. Includes goosegrass and crosswort as well as all the bedstraws.

Borage family *Boraginaceae*
Annual or perennial herbs often roughly hairy. Flowers for the most part blue, sometimes pink in bud; 5 fused sepals and petals usually growing in a 1-sided spike, generally tightly coiled in bud. Includes forget-me-nots and comfrey as well as borage.

Bindweed family *Convolvulaceae*
Herbaceous annuals or perennials with twining stems, usually in an anti-clockwise direction. Leaves undivided and untoothed. Characterised by large trumpet-shaped flowers that are pink or white.

Nightshade family *Solanaceae*
Annual, herbaceous perennials or shrubs. Leaves usually alternate, without stipules. Flowers solitary, usually actinomorphic with 5 sepals and 5 petals fused into a tube. Represented in Westerdale by a single thorn-apple.

Ash family *Oleaceae*
Trees, shrubs or woody scramblers, leaves opposite, entire to serrated. Flowers usually in dense clusters with 2 stamens, 4 fused sepals and 4-6 fused petals. Fruit a 2-valved capsule. Represented in Westerdale by ash and lilac.

Speedwell family *Veronicaceae*
Herbaceous annuals or perennials; part of the former figwort family. Flowers with 4 or 5 petals joined at the base, some such as the toadflaxes and foxglove with tubular flowers. Speedwells themselves have 4 petals, two matching at the sides, one larger upper petal and one narrower at the base, with two protruding stamens.

Plantain family *Plantaginaceae*
Annual or perennial largely green herbs. Leaves with parallel veins in a basal rosette; shape important for identification. Flowers in a dense spike, flower parts in sets of 4 with prominent stamens.

Water-starwort family *Callitrichaceae*
Annual or perennial herbs growing in water or on mud. Stems thread-like. Identifiable by narrow leaves growing opposite each other along the stem. Leaves floating or submerged. Flowers monoecious, green, *without* petals or sepals, male a single stamen, female a 4-celled ovary, on the same plant. Only common water-starwort found in Westerdale; seen as green cover on still water.

Figwort family *Scrophulariaceae*
Herbaceous annuals, biennials or perennials, some with square stems. Family characterised by a 2-lobed ovary and 2 many-seeded cells (see dead-nettle family below). Flowers variable. A family that has been much re-classified due to modern molecular analysis. Includes great mullein as well as common figwort.

Dead-nettle family *Lamiaceae*
Herbaceous annuals or perennials often aromatic and with characteristic square stems and opposite leaves. Leaves usually stalked and undivided. Flowers zygomorphic having 5 sepals fused to form teeth and 5 unequal petals fused into a tube. With 4-lobed ovary and 4 single-seeded nutlets (see figwort family above). Formerly *Labiatae*, plants in this family still referred to as labiates. Includes betony, mints and ground-ivy as well as the dead-nettles.

Monkeyflower family *Phrymaceae*
Herbaceous perennials with leafy stolons. Stems round, leaves sessile without stipules. Flowers zygomorphic in terminal raceme. Calyx with 5 lobes usually fused, corolla with 2 upper and 3 lower lobes. Easily recognised as water-side plants with striking yellow flowers.

Includes all the *Mimulus* species but only *M. moschatus* found in Westerdale.

Broomrape family *Orobanchaceae*
A family of parasitic and semi-parasitic plants also once part of the figwort family. The semi-parasitic plants have green leaves, unlike the true parasites of the genus *Orobanche,* but parasitise the roots of host plants for water and minerals. Includes eyebright and cow-wheat.

Holly family *Aquifoliaceae*
Unmistakable evergreen trees or shrubs, leaves with spiny margins. Flowers small, white, usually dioecious, with 4 sepals and 4 petals. Male flowers with 4 stamens, female flowers with 4-celled ovary. Fruit a drupe.

Bellflower family *Campanulaceae*
Herbaceous annuals or, more usually, perennials. Leaves undivided and alternate. Flowers usually blue, occasionally white, in characteristic bell shape having 5 fused petals. Family represented only by harebell in Westerdale.

Daisy family *Asteraceae*
Formerly *Compositae,* the largest of the plant families. Herbaceous annuals or perennials. Flowers massed into a tight head known as a capitulum; individual flowers known as florets. Inner disc florets with 5 fused petals, outer ray florets ending in a flat strap known as a ligule. Composite flowers are of three types – daisy-type with inner yellow disc florets surrounded by ray florets; thistle-type with disc florets only; dandelion-type with ray florets only (usually yellow). Flowers held within sepal-like bracts collectively called the involucre; shape and size of these helps identification. Fruits often have a 'parachute' of fine hairs known as a pappus. Includes all of the familiar daisies, dandelions and thistles as well as yarrow, ragwort, groundsel, knapweed and winter heliotrope.

Honeysuckle family *Caprifoliaceae*
Deciduous or evergreen shrubs or woody climbers. Flowers very variable. Includes elder and viburnum as well as the familiar honeysuckle.

Valerian family *Valerianaceae*
Annual or perennial herbs. Leaves without stipules. Flowers with 1 or 3 stamens and 5 petals fused into a tube, in domed head or panicle. Family represented here solely by common valerian.

Teasel family *Dipsacaceae*
Biennial or perennial herbs very similar to the daisy family (see above). Leaves opposite along the stem. Flowers in a dense flower head, a capitulum, looking as if they are large single flowers. Flowers with 4 separate stamens, bristle-like sepals and 4 or 5 joined petals. Whole flower sits within a cup of green bracts. Includes scabious as well as teasel.

Ivy family *Araliaceae*
Evergreen woody climbers, herbaceous perennials or deciduous shrubs. Leaves alternate, usually simple, without stipules. Flowers white to greenish in characteristic terminal umbel, with 5 petals and 5 stamens. Fruit usually a black berry with 2-5 seeds.

Pennywort family *Hydrocotylaceae*
Herbaceous low growing perennials that root at the leaf nodes. Flowers with 5 sepals and 5 petals growing in umbels. Very similar to umbellifers proper but much lower growing and with stipules. Represented in Westerdale by marsh pennywort, rarely seen in flower.

Carrot family *Apiaceae*
Herbaceous annuals or perennials. Leaves often divided and feathery. Flowers usually white, 5 petals, on stalks, forming a flat or domed umbrella-like head. Collectively known as umbellifers. Shape of fruits and presence of bracts or bracteoles aid identification. Includes hogweed and cow parsley.

MONOCOTYLEDONS – plants with single seed leaves following germination.

Arum family *Araceae*
Herbaceous perennials with underground tubers or rhizomes. An unusual family of plants with tightly packed flowers, male above the female, around a cylindrical spadix held within a leaf-like structure known as the spathe. NOTE all arum plants are **very poisonous**, especially the berries. Only wild arum or 'lords and ladies' (*Arum maculatum*) found in Westerdale.

Arrowgrass family *Juncaginaceae*
Rhizomatous perennials with leafless flowering stems, leaves in a basal rosette. Flowers inconspicuous, 6 tepals in simple terminal raceme. Prefers damp acidic conditions. Only marsh arrowgrass (*Triglochin palustris*) found in Westerdale.

Pondweed family *Potamogetonaceae*
Hairless, aquatic annuals or perennials with leafy, submerged flowering stems. Leaves floating and/or submerged. Flowers in short spikes from leaf axils, often inconspicuous. Only bog pondweed (*Potamogeton polygonifolius*) found in Westerdale.

Bog asphodel family *Nartheciaceae*
Erect, hairless, rhizomatous perennials with mostly basal, spear-like leaves. Actinomorphic flowers in terminal racemes with 6 tepals and 6 stamens and a single style. A family solely represented throughout the country by bog asphodel (*Narthecium ossifragum*).

Orchid family *Orchidaceae*
Upright herbaceous perennials growing from an underground tuber or rhizome. Leaves usually basal, undivided and untoothed, sometimes with dark spots. Flowers usually in a spike with 3, sometimes coloured, sepals and with leaf-like bracts to each spike. Flower shapes very variable but with 2 lips; shape of lower lip or labellum is an important aid to identification. Fruits egg-shaped or cylindrical, seeds many and minute; need the presence of mycorrhizal fungi for germination. Hybrids frequent, which makes identification difficult. Four species found in Westerdale.

Daffodil family *Amaryllidaceae*
Formerly onion family (*Alliaceae*). Herbaceous perennials growing from a bulb, corm or rhizome. *Allium* species all smell strongly of garlic. Leaves usually narrow, except for ramsons, all with parallel veins. Flowers solitary or in umbel-like head. Includes snowdrops and ramsons as well as daffodils.

Asparagus family *Asparagaceae*
A diverse family of plants including evergreen shrubs as well as herbaceous perennials some of which grow from a bulb. Common features are flowers similar to the lily family with 6 tepals and 6 stamens. This family as a whole includes the agaves, cordylines, yuccas and asparagus, lily of the valley and, as here in Westerdale, bluebells.

Rush family *Juncaceae*

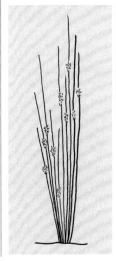

Rush flower

Herbaceous, usually perennial plants with largely cylindrical leaves and stems – rushes are round, sedges have edges – and inconspicuous flowers. Florets made up of six perianth segments,

Fruit

aka tepals, and 3 or 6 stamens. Flowers arranged in terminal inflorescence sometimes appearing to grow from the side of the stem. Includes rushes and wood-rushes.

Sedge family *Cyperaceae*

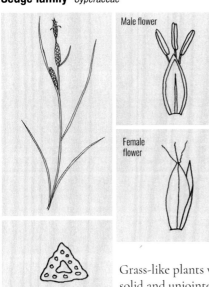

Male flower

Female flower

Grass-like plants with solid and unjointed stems usually triangular in cross section. Sedges have edges. Leaves usually borne in three vertical ranks up the stem and consist of blade, sheath and ligule. Length and orientation of bracts an aid to identification. The sedge family includes club-rushes, spike-rushes and cottongrasses as well as the true sedges, *Carex* species. In true sedges the flowers are in spikes, upper spike usually (but not always) entirely male, lower usually (but not always) entirely female; the female flowers have an extra inner glume, the flask- or bottle-shaped utricle, which encloses the fruit. Note: *Carex* species can be easier to identify in fruit than in flower.

Grass family *Poaceae*

Grass spikelet

Parts of a grass flower

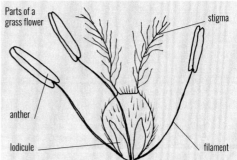

stigma

anther

lodicule

filament

Familiar herbaceous plants with hollow stems and leaves arising from swollen nodes. Leaves consist of blade and sheath with a papery ligule at the base. Size and shape of the ligule is an important aid to identification (lens needed to view). Inflorescence made up of spikelets comprising 2 glumes enclosing the lemma and palea, which in turn enclose the flower parts.

For further information see Rose's *Grasses, Sedges, Rushes and Ferns of the British Isles and north-western Europe*; *Collins Flower Guide* and Stace's *New Flora of the British Isles*.

White flowers

DICOTYLEDONS

Poppy family *Papaveraceae*

Climbing corydalis *Ceratocapnos claviculata*

A delicate scrambling annual up to 75cm, found on moorland often under bracken. Leaves slender, greyish, ending in tendrils. Flowers 4-6mm, creamy white, in clusters May-Sept.

Buttercup family *Ranunculaceae*

Round-leaved crowfoot *Ranunculus omiophyllus*

Aka water crowfoot. An aquatic plant found trailing on wet mud and in acidic pools and ditches. Leaves rounded, divided into 3-5 lobes. Flowers 10-12mm with moon-shaped honey guides on each of 5 white petals which cover the down-turned sepals, March-Oct.

Wood anemone *Anemone nemorosa*

Aka lady's nightcap and wind flower. Perennial to 30 cm, forms a white carpet in spring, an indicator of ancient, deciduous woodland. Leaves much divided, 3 leaf-like bracts below flowers. Flowers 20-30mm, solitary, white but often flushed with pink, with 5-8 *sepals* and no petals, March-May.

Stonecrop family *Crassulaceae*

White stonecrop *Sedum album*

Low growing to 20cm. Leaves alternate along stem, sometimes tinged red. Flowers 6-9mm, June-Aug.

Pea family *Fabaceae*

White clover *Trifolium repens*

Familiar lawn weed. Spreading perennial to 50cm. Leaflets toothed with white marks. Flower head 15-20mm on long stalk, May-Nov.

17

Milkwort family *Polygalaceae*

Heath milkwort *Polygala serpyllifolia*

Slender hairless perennial to 30cm. Leaves lanceolate, unstalked and fairly crowded along stem, lower leaves *opposite*. Flowers 5-6mm of unusual shape appearing to have 5 petals but with 3 outer sepals and 2 petal-like sepals folded out like wings over the 3 tiny fringed petals, May-Sept. Usually blue or mauve only occasionally white, see also under section on blue flowers.

Rose family *Rosaceae*

Meadowsweet *Filipendula ulmaria*

Aka queen of the meadow. Sturdy hairless perennial to 1m tall, found in damp places. Leaves silvery beneath. Flowers in frothy creamy-white clusters, 4-8mm, *very fragrant*, June-Sept.

Sacred to the Druids and formerly used as a strewing herb (to strew on earth floors), a favourite of Elizabeth I, also used for bridal garlands hence once known as bridewort. In the 1830s meadowsweet was found to be a source of salicylic acid from which aspirin was later synthesised.

Barren strawberry *Potentilla sterilis*

Hairy perennial to 15cm. Leaves trifoliate with spreading hairs beneath, end tooth of terminal leaflet shorter than others. Flowers white *with gaps between petals*, Feb-May.

Wood-sorrel family *Oxalidaceae*

Wood sorrel *Oxalis acetosella*

Leaves bright green, shamrock-like with three rounded leaflets. Flowers 12-18mm, white with mauve veins and yellow centres, May-Sept.

Flax family *Linaceae*

Fairy flax *Linum catharticum*

Slender, delicate annual to 25cm. Flowers 4-6mm, having 5 petals with yellow centres, May-Sept.

Cabbage family *Brassicaceae*

Garlic mustard *Alliaria petiolata*

Aka Jack by the hedge, a common hedgerow weed. Variable up to 120cm. Smells like garlic when crushed. Leaves bright green, stalked and somewhat heart-shaped. Flowers 5-7mm, April-June. Seed pods cylindrical, 4-angled, held upright. Former culinary and medicinal herb.

Shepherd's purse *Capsella bursa-pastoris*

Aka shovelweed, a common garden weed. Downy annual to 50cm. Leaves variable. Flowers 2-3mm, Jan-Dec. Characterised by its flattened seed pods said to look like a shepherd's satchel.

Field penny-cress *Thlaspi arvense*

Hairless foetid annual to 60cm. Leaves yellowish, shiny and toothed, clasping stem, with rounded lobes. Flowers white with yellow anthers, 4-6mm, May-Sept. Fruit a circular pod with broad wings, notched at top looking penny-like, hence its common name. An arable weed thus much less frequent now. See also under section on green plants.

Large bittercress *Cardamine armara*

Perennial with creeping stems to 60cm rooting at nodes. Found in damp shady places. Leaves pale green without basal rosette. Flowers 11-13mm, usually white, anthers violet, May-June. Seed pods cylindrical. Not to be confused with lady's smock (*Cardamine pratensis*) qv.

Hairy bittercress *Cardamine hirsuta*

Annual to 30cm but usually much shorter. Leaves hairy above, stem leaflets narrower than rounded basal ones. Flowers 2-3mm with 4 stamens , Feb-Nov. Pods narrow, extending beyond flowers.

Wavy bittercress *Cardamine flexuosa*

Usually biennial, likes muddy sites. Slightly zig-zag stems up to 50cm. Flowers very small with six stamens, April-Sept.

Dame's violet *Hesperis matronalis*

Aka sweet rocket and dame's gillyflower. Sturdy perennial to 1m. Leaves *lanceolate* and toothed. Fruit a long cylindrical pod. Flowers 15-20mm, very fragrant, with four petals, white or varying shades of lilac, May-Aug. The dame refers to Damascus; *Hesperis* is from the Greek for evening as the scent is most pronounced then. At one time known as vesper flowers because of their evening scent, when vesper prayers were said in church. Not to be confused with honesty *qv*. See also under section on red, pink and purple flowers.

Sundew family *Droseraceae*

Round-leaved sundew *Drosera rotundifolia*

Insectivorous perennial with rosette of basal leaves. Leaves rounded, sharply narrowed into downy stalks. Flower stalks leafless to 10cm, flowers small with 5 white petals, June-Aug.

Pink family *Caryophyllaceae*

Thyme-leaved sandwort *Arenaria serpyllifolia*

Easily missed, slender annual to 25cm. Leaves hairy. Flowers very small, petals shorter than sepals with 10 stamens and 3 styles, June-Aug.

Bog stitchwort *Stellaria alsine*

Considered to be a plant intermediate between true stitchworts and chickweeds. A prostrate perennial preferring acidic marshy ground. Square stem, smooth and slender, up to 40cm. Leaves oval and pointed, mostly sessile; narrow bracts with green mid-rib. Flowers 5-7mm, *petals shorter than sepals*, May-Sept.

Greater stitchwort *Stellaria holostea*

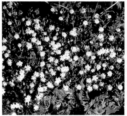 

The most robust of the stitchworts with the largest flowers. Stems up to 60cm, rough edged with four distinct angles. Leaves sessile. Petals longer than sepals and deeply cleft with rounded lobes. Flowers 15-30mm, March-June.

Lesser stitchwort *Stellaria graminea*

Smallest flowered of the true stitchworts. Stems up to 80cm with smooth angles. Flowers 5-12mm, with deeply cut, *pointed* petals, March-May.

Wood stitchwort   *Stellaria nemorum*

More like a chickweed than a stitchwort; likes damp shady places. Stems up to 60cm, slightly hairy especially at leaf nodes. Petals twice as long as sepals. Flowers 10-18mm, May-Aug. This species is very rare in the vice-county so an interesting find in Westerdale.

Chickweed   *Stellaria media*

A common and familiar garden weed. Prostrate sprawling annual up to 50cm. Two lines of hairs opposite each other along stem. Sepals downy with pale margins. Petals very small and deeply notched, usually shorter than sepals. Flowers 5-9mm, Jan-Dec. Leaves edible, at one time used in salads.

Common mouse-ear   *Cerastium fontanum*

Erect or sprawling perennial to 50cm, hairy with some leafy non-flowering shoots. Sepals and bracts with pale, narrow margins. Petals may be longer or shorter than sepals. Flowers 6-10mm, April-Nov.

Sticky mouse-ear   *Cerastium glomeratum*

Low growing, stickily hairy, to 45cm. Sepals with long hairs and narrow pale edges. Flowers small, 5-8mm, rarely fully opening, in distinctive compact flower head, April-Oct.

White campion   *Silene latifolia*

Usually annual to 1m. Leaves lanceolate, lower leaves with unwinged stalks. Flowers 25-30mm, with 5 cleft petals, *calyx pale green*, May-Oct. Not to be confused with a white-flowered red campion, which has a dark, brownish red calyx. Hybridises with red campion qv.

Corn spurrey   *Spergula arvensis*

Straggly, stickily hairy annual to 40cm. Leaves greyish, furrowed below, growing in whorls around stem. Flowers 4-7mm, with 5 *styles*, petals un-notched, April-Sept.

Primrose family *Primulaceae*

Chickweed-wintergreen *Trientalis europaea*

Delicate perennial to 50cm found on moorland, often hidden under bracken. Leaves pale green in a whorl around stem. Flowers single on slender stalk, 15-18mm with 5-9 petals, May-Aug.

Towards the south-eastern limit of its range.

Bedstraw family *Rubiaceae*

Goosegrass *Galium aparine*

Aka sweethearts, cleavers and sitcky willie. Troublesome hedgerow weed resistant to many herbicides, often scrambling to 3m. Catches on animal fur or people's clothing due to many curved prickles. Leaves in whorls along stem, wider towards tip, ending in a minute bristle. Flowers inconspicuous, 1-2mm, May-Sept. See also under section on green plants.

Hedge bedstraw *Galium album*

More robust than heath or fen bedstraw. Scrambling perennial with smooth square stem to 1.5m. Elliptical leaves in whorls of 6-8 with *forward pointing* prickles along edges and short end point. Flowers 2-5mm, in clusters, with pointed petals, June-Sept.

Heath bedstraw *Galium saxatile*

Low growing hairless perennial to 30cm. Leaves in whorls of 5-8, sharply pointed with *forward pointing* prickles along edges. Flowers very small, only 3mm, in clusters, May-Aug.

Fen bedstraw *Galium uliginosum*

Stems to 60cm with *down-turned* prickles. Leaves narrow with minute bristle at tip (need to use lens), *backward pointing* prickles along leaf edges, 5-8 per whorl. Flowers 2-3mm in loose clusters, June-Aug. Fruits with low-domed warts.

Marsh bedstraw   *Galium palustre*

Variable, hairless perennial with rough stems to 1m. Leaves in whorls of 4-5, *blunt* with prickles along edges. Flowers 2-4mm in loose clusters, June-Aug.

Bindweed family   *Convolvulaceae*

Hedge bindweed   *Calystegia sepium*

Hairless climber to 2m. Leaves arrow-shaped. Flowers white trumpets, 3-4cm across, sepals only partly covered by two large bracts, June-Sept.

Nightshade family   *Solanaceae*

Thorn-apple   *Datura stramonium*

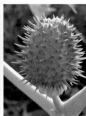

Aka jimsonweed. Distinctive, erect annual to 1m. Leaves ovate, deeply and jaggedly toothed. Flowers trumpet-shaped, July-Oct. Fruits ovoid, large and spiny giving the plant its common name. Poisonous.

Dead-nettle family   *Lamiaceae*

White dead-nettle   *Lamium album*

Aka white archangel. Familiar roadside weed. Creeping perennial to 60cm. Leaves heart-shaped similar to nettles but without stinging hairs. Open-mouthed flowers tinged with green on lower lip, 18-25mm, March-Nov. The black anthers are said to resemble slippers – country children believed that the fairies left them there after they had finished dancing.

Common hemp-nettle   *Galeopsis tetrahit*

Easily missed annual with bristly stems to 1m. Flowers usually creamy white, sometimes pink, with dark markings on *rounded* lower lip, 13-20mm, July-Sept. Not to be confused with bifid hemp-nettle (*Galeopsis bifida*) qv.

Broomrape family *Orobanchaceae*

Common eyebright *Euphrasia nemorosa*

Low growing, semi-parasitic annual found along moorland lane edges. Leaves small and serrated. Flowers white with mauve veining, 5-8mm, May-Sept. Once used as a treatment for eye complaints, hence its common name. As well as tannins, eyebrights have been found to contain iridoid glycosides, which do heal the membranes of the eye.

Daisy family *Asteraceae*

Daisy *Bellis perennis*

The 'day's eye' as flowers close as the sun goes down, the ubiquitous lawn weed familiar to all. Leaves in low growing rosette. Flowers 12-15mm, on hairy stems; white ray florets often tipped with red, Jan-Dec.

Ox eye daisy *Leucanthemum vulgare*

Aka moon daisy or marguerite. Unbranched perennial to 75cm. Leaves spoon-shaped on long stalks, upper leaves clasping the stem. Flowers solitary, 25-60mm, May-Sept.

Feverfew *Tanecetum parthenium*

Downy perennial to 70cm with bitter smell. Flowers with short ray florets, June-Sept. As its common name suggests, this has been used as a healing plant for centuries and is still used as an effective treatment for migraine.

Scentless mayweed *Tripleurospermum inodorum*

Sprawling, hairless, non-aromatic annual to 60cm. Leaves much divided, feathery with short bristle at tip. Flowers 30-45mm, with characteristic brown edges to sepal-like bracts, April-Nov.

Yarrow *Achillea millefolium*

Downy perennial to 80cm. Leaves dark green, deeply divided and feathery. Flowers usually white, sometimes tinged pink, 4-6mm in a flat umbel-like head, June-Dec. Considered sacred by the Druids and used for many centuries as a medicinal herb especially for staunching wounds.

Sneezewort *Achillea ptarmica*

Greyish perennial to 60cm. Leaves linear, pointed with fine teeth. Flowers 12-18mm, in loose clusters, centres greenish white, July-Sept. The leaves of this plant were dried and used as a type of snuff, hence its common name.

Valerian family *Valerianaceae*

Common valerian *Valeriana officinalis*

Unbranched perennial to 2m. Leaves pinnate with narrow leaflets, may be toothed or untoothed. Flowers fragrant, sometimes pale pink, 4-5mm with 5 petals, June-Aug. Used in herbal medicine throughout the world. During both World Wars used as a treatment for shell shock and other nervous conditions.

Carrot family *Apiaceae*

Cow parsley *Anthriscus sylvestris*

Aka bad man's oatmeal and Queen Anne's lace; a familiar roadside weed. A downy perennial to 1m, stem *hollow*. Flowers in frothy white umbels 20-60mm, April-June. Fruits smooth, broader at base than at tip.

Hedge parsley *Torilis japonica*

Aka upright hedge parsley. Similar to cow parsley but later flowering and tends to grow further back on grass verge. Annual to 1m, stems *solid* with short prickly hairs which can be felt by running fingers *down* the stem. Flowers pinkish white in umbels 20-40mm, July-Sept. Fruits egg-shaped with purple hooked bristles. Not to be confused with cow parsley or rough chervil *qv*.

Rough chervil *Chaerophyllum temulum*

Flowering time between cow parsley and hedge parsley. Solid, purple-spotted stem to 1m, swollen at leaf nodes. Coarsely hairy biennial. Whole plant turns purple after flowering. Flowers in umbels 30-60mm, May-July. Fruits burgundy coloured and ridged.

Sweet cicely *Myrris odorata*

Distinctive aromatic perennial to 1m. Leaves bright green, with characteristic white markings, smelling of aniseed when bruised. Leaves sometimes still used to sweeten rhubarb to avoid using too much sugar. Flowers in frothy umbels 10-60mm, April-June. Fruits upright, ribbed and shiny, green at first, ripening to dark brown. During the Middle Ages, ripe fruits were collected and dried and chewed to ward off hunger pangs, also used to flavour Chartreuse liqueur.

Hogweed *Heracleum sphondylium*

Robust plant taller than other common umbellifers. Hollow ridged stem to 2m or more, roughly hairy. Flowers usually white, sometimes pink, in umbels 5-20cm, May-Nov. Fruits flattened, oval with dark streaks. Formerly used for animal fodder, hence its common name, also a medicinal herb. The stems are hollow and at onc time were used by country children as pea shooters. Not to be confused with giant hogweed (*Heracleum mantegazzianum*) which grows *much* taller, is a pernicious invader and, thankfully, not found in Westerdale.

Pignut *Conopodiuim majus*

Most delicate looking of the umbellifers found here. Slender, hairless perennial to 40cm. Grows from a tuber liked by pigs, hence its common name. Pointed leaves deeply divided, hairy along edges. Flowers in umbels 30-70mm, May-July. Fruits oval with persistent styles. An indicator of old grassland. Attempts were once made to grow this on a commercial scale for animal fodder but these were unsuccessful on improved land.

Wild carrot *Daucus carota* ssp *carota*

Bg 2014. Hairy biennial with *conspicuous bracts* below flowers. Stems solid to 1.5m. Flowers in umbels 30-70mm often with beetroot-red centre, June-Sept. Fruits with hooked spines.

Ground-elder *Aegopodium podagraria*

Hairless perennial with hollow creeping stems to 1m, forming dense patches. Leaves variable with irregularly toothed leaflets. Flowers in umbels 20-60mm, *no bracts*, June-Aug. Fruits egg-shaped and ribbed. Brought by the Romans as a culinary and medicinal herb. Can become a pernicious garden weed.

Wild angelica *Angelica sylvestris*

Tall, sturdy perennial to 2.5m liking damp places. Ridged, purplish stem. Leaves pinnate, leaflets with serrated edges. Flowers without bracts, in umbels 30-150mm across, often tinged with pink, June-Sept. Fruits oval with four wings. Not to be confused with garden angelica (*Angelica archangelica*) which is not found in the wild in Westerdale. It is garden angelica that is used for the sweetmeat for cake decoration.

MONOCOTYLEDONS

Daffodil family *Amaryllidaceae*

Ramsons *Allium ursinum*

Aka wild garlic. Leaves broad, tapering to a point and strongly smelling of garlic. Flowers 12-20mm, star-like with 5 *tepals*, April-June.

Snowdrop *Galanthus nivalis*

Aka fair maids of February, the harbingers of spring. Growing from a bulb, to 20cm. Leaves in pairs, slender, greyish green. Flowers 12-25mm, bell-shaped, solitary with 3 pure white outer tepals and 3 inner ones with green markings towards the tip, Jan-March.

Double snowdrop *Galanthus nivalis flore pleno*

Similar to a single snowdrop but with 6 outer tepals – 3 pure white, 3 with central green veining – and an inner 'frilly petticoat' of white tepals with green markings, Jan-March.

Snowdrops are also known as snow piercers as that is what they do. They possess anti-freeze proteins that inhibit the formation of ice crystals even in the coldest weather thus the plants are protected from cell damage.

Yellow flowers

Poppy family *Papaveraceae*

Greater celandine *Chelidonium majus*

Aka swallow-wort. Perennial to 85cm. Leaves pale green with rounded lobes. Flowers bright yellow with 4 rounded petals, 15-25mm, April-Oct. Fruit a long cylindrical capsule. Usually found growing along walls close to habitation. Cultivated since Anglo-Saxon times as a medicinal herb. Not to be confused with lesser celandine *qv*.

Welsh poppy *Mecanopsis cambrica*

Slightly hairy perennial to 60cm. Leaves scented, pale green, divided into toothed leaflets. Flowers occasionally orange, solitary on tall unbranched stems, 5-7cm, May-Oct. Fruit a long oval capsule with short beak. Garden escape remaining close to habitation.

Buttercup family *Ranunculaceae*

Creeping buttercup *Ranunculus repens*

Perennial with creeping runners rooting at nodes, found in grassland. Whole plant 40-60cm, but appears shorter. Leaves, hairy, roughly triangular with 3 deeply cut lobes, end one on *long stalk*. Familiar glossy yellow buttercup flowers 20-30mm, on *furrowed* stalks, May-Oct, sometimes for longer if mild.

Meadow buttercup *Ranunculus acris*

Tallest of the buttercups, 80-100cm. Hairy perennial. Leaves palmate, deeply cut with end lobe *unstalked*. Flowers glossy yellow, 15-25mm, on *unfurrowed* stalks, April-Oct. Fruits glabrous achenes.

Lesser spearwort *Ranunculus flammula*

Perennial to 50cm found in wet places. Leaves long and narrow, very slightly toothed. Flowers glossy yellow, 7-20mm, June-Oct.

Marsh marigold *Caltha palustris*

Aka king cups and May blobs. Hairless perennial growing along stream sides. Fleshy stems to 60cm. Leaves kidney-shaped, dark green and glossy, on long stalks. Flowers like large buttercups but with 5-8 shiny yellow sepals (tepals) and *no petals*, 10-50mm, March-June.

Lesser celandine *Ficaria verna*

Formerly *Ranunculus ficaria*. One of the earliest of our spring flowers, not to be confused with greater celandine *qv*. Hairless perennial to 30cm. Leaves dark green, sometimes mottled with white markings, heart-shaped on long stalks. Flowers solitary, 10-30mm with 7-12 narrow glossy yellow petals, greyish beneath. This plant used to be known as pilewort as it was used as a treatment for haemorrhoids. Two subspecies: *Ficaria verna* ssp *verna* is less common and has bulbils in leaf axils, sometimes seen along hedgerows or the base of walls, occasionally marking former boundaries. *Ficaria verna* ssp *fertilis* has no bulbils and produces ripe seeds, more characteristic of disturbed ground and gardens, March-May.

Saxifrage family *Saxifragaceae*

Opposite-leaved golden saxifrage
Chrysosplenium oppositifolium

Low creeping perennial with *square* stems to 15cm, mat-forming in damp patches. Leaves rounded, bluntly toothed, on *opposite* sides of stem. Flowers 3-4mm, *without petals*, with yellowish-green sepals and bracts and bright yellow anthers, Feb-July. Found by stream-sides and other wet places. See also under section on green plants.

Pea family *Fabaceae*

Meadow vetchling *Lathyrus pratensis*

Scrambling perennial to 1.5m but often much shorter. Leaves narrow, in pairs along stem with arrow-shaped stipules and curling tendrils. Flowers 10-18mm, 5-12 growing together in short spike, May-Aug. Pods black.

Black medick *Medicago lupulina*

Sprawling annual or short-lived perennial to 60cm. Leaves downy with toothed leaflets *ending in a minute point* (use a hand lens to view). Flowers bright yellow in tightly packed head, 3-6mm, with *hairy* sepals, April-Oct. Fruits coiled and black. Not to be confused with lesser trefoil.

Lesser trefoil *Trifolium dubium*

Hairless sprawling annual to 25cm. Leaves with notched leaflets *without* terminal point, middle leaflet on long stalk. Flowers dull yellow, 10-20 in loose head with *hairless*, joined sepals, May-Sept. Not to be confused with black medick.

Bird's foot trefoil *Lotus corniculatus*

Sparsely hairy, usually creeping perennial with *solid* stems to 50cm. Leaves with 3 leaflets, lower pair bent back along stem. Flowers 10-16mm, 2-7 in head, deep yellow tipped with red and orange hence aka bacon and eggs, May-Sept. Fruits long pods looking like an outstretched hand hence aka ladies' fingers. *Prefers dry roadsides.*

Greater bird's foot trefoil *Lotus pedunculatus*

Larger than above species, stems stouter and *hollow* to 1m. Leaves bluish green. Flowers dull yellow, 5-12 in head, sepal teeth spread in bud, 2 upper ones at an acute angle, June-Aug. Fruits long pods 13-35mm. *Prefers damp marshy ground.*

Bush vetch, sport *Vicia sepium*

Scrambling perennial to 60cm. Leaves with 5-8 pairs of leaflets and branching tendrils. Pods hairless, 20-35mm, blackening as they ripen. Flowers gingerish at first, opening to be a creamy white, 12-15mm, 2-6 on short-stalked head, April-Nov. Flowers usually purple but this yellow form or 'sport' seen just occasionally, see also under purple flowers.

Rose family *Rosaceae*

Herb bennet *Geum urbanum*

Aka wood avens and, formerly, the holy herb *herba benedicta*. Common perennial often found in woodland. Stems hairy to 70cm. Leaves on long stalks, lower leaves with long end lobe. Significant leaf-like stipules. Flowers 8-15mm with spaces between the 5 rounded petals, 5 sepals turning downwards as the flowers open, May-Nov. Fruits in bur-like head with hooked styles remaining to aid seed dispersal. In medieval times the roots, which are aromatic when crushed, were used against the plague. Sadly this plant has no healing properties.

Silverweed *Potentilla anserina*

Silvery leaves make this species unmistakable. Prostrate perennial with long runners to 80cm. Leaves pinnate with alternate large and small well-toothed leaflets, sometimes silvery on both sides, sometimes on underside only, never on the upper side only but occasionally on neither side! Flowers 15-20mm, *solitary*, on long stalks, May-Aug. Often seen along roadsides. Before the introduction of the potato in the sixteenth century, silverweed was an important crop plant, its starchy root boiled or baked or used to make bread or porridge.

Tormentil *Potentilla erecta*

Creeping perennial preferring acid soil; found on moorland. Leaves usually with 3 toothed leaflets appearing as 5 due to leaf-like stipules. Flowers with 4 petals, 7-11mm, May-Sept. Roots provide a red dye formerly used in tanning.

Creeping cinquefoil *Potentilla reptans*

Low growing perennial with rooting runners to 1m seen along road verges. Leaves on long stalks, palmate with 3-5 leaflets. Flowers solitary with 5 bright yellow petals, 17-25mm growing from leaf axils on long slender stalks, June-Sept.

Cinquefoil hybrid *P anglica x P reptans = P x mixta*

A hybrid of trailing tormentil and creeping cinquefoil usually in the absence of the rare parent plant *Potentilla anglica*. Distinguished by having leaves with 3 or 4 leaflets and flowers with 4 or 5 petals *on the same plant.*

Pale lady's mantle *Alchemilla xanthochlora*

Low growing perennial similar to the garden lady's mantle (*Alchemilla mollis*). Easily identified by leaves, which are palmately lobed with straight pointed teeth and very few hairs on upper surface. Flowers in loose clusters, only 2-3mm, with 2 rings of sepals, *no petals* and yellow anthers, June-Aug. There are 15 species of lady's mantle, only one grows in Westerdale.

The botanical name *Alchemilla* is from the Arabic *alkemelych* from which we get the word alchemy. This plant was regarded as the Little Alchemist, believed to have healing properties. Its habit of guttation also gave it magical attributes. Its common name refers to its cloak-like appearance, at one time called Our Lady's mantle with reference to the Virgin Mary. It was regarded as 'a woman's best friend' as it was used for menstrual and menopausal problems.

Violet family *Violaceae*

Field pansy *Viola arvensis*

Low growing, much branched annual. Stipules toothed and leaf-like. Flowers small, familiar pansy form with *petals shorter than sepals,* sepals showing between the petals, April-Oct. Can be varying shades of yellow or mauve.

St John's wort family *Hypericaceae*

Slender St John's wort *Hypericum pulchrum*

Hairless, slender perennial on smooth stems to 60cm. Leaves heart-shaped, slightly clasping stem, with translucent dots and rolled over edges (use hand lens to view). Flowers rich yellow, red beneath and edged with black dots, 12-18mm, June-Aug.

Square-stemmed St John's wort *Hypericum tetrapterum*

Aka square-stalked St John's wort. Hairless perennial with winged stems to 60cm. Leaves with translucent dots. Flowers 9-13mm, with pointed sepals and pale yellow petals, *usually without* black dots, July-Sept. Grows in very damp conditions.

Trailing St John's wort *Hypericum humifusum*

Prostrate perennial with thin stems to 20cm, prefers acid soil. Stems with 2 ridges. Leaves pale green with black and translucent dots. Flowers with few black dots, 8-12mm, petals at least twice as long as sepals, June-Sept.

Marsh St John's wort *Hypericum elodes*

Perennial with sprawling, rooting red stems to 40cm. Leaves rounded, so hairy they appear greyish. Flowers 12-20mm, yellow fringed with red dots, usually not fully opening, June-Sept. Prefers very wet, acidic conditions; a rare plant in the vice-county.

Cabbage family *Brassicaceae*

Hedge mustard *Sisymbrium officinale*

Annual, sometimes biennial, with stiff stems to 1m, growing in candelabra-like fashion. A common wayside weed. Leaves deeply lobed at base, clasping stem in upper part of plant. Flowers, just 3mm, clustered at tips of stems, April-Oct. Fruits lie close to stem.

Charlock *Sinapis arvensis*

Erect, coarse annual to 1m. Leaves bristly, roughly lobed and toothed, lower stalked, upper sessile. Flowers 15-20mm with 4 bright yellow petals, sepals spreading or down-turned, April-Nov. Fruit a cylindrical pod with rounded beak.

Primrose family *Primulaceae*

Primrose *Primula vulgaris*

Perennial with basal rosette of crinkly leaves tapering into stalk. Flowers 20-40mm, pale yellow with darker centres, solitary on long leafless stalks (scapes), fragrant, March-May. Leaves once used for culinary and medicinal purposes.

Cowslip *Primula veris*

Aka the keys of St Peter. Attractive perennial to 30cm, whole plant softly hairy. Leaves crinkled, sharply contracted towards base. Flowers tubular, in umbels on leafless stalk, characteristic orange spot at base of petals, April-May. Fruit a capsule enclosed by remaining calyx. Traditionally used for cowslip wine.

Yellow pimpernel *Lysimachia nemorum*

Hairless, low growing perennial to 40cm forming patches in woodland. Pointed leaves in opposite pairs. Flowers 5-8mm, star-like, opening in fine weather, May-Aug.

Bedstraw family *Rubiaceae*

Lady's bedstraw *Galium verum*

Spreading perennial to 1m. Narrow, hairless leaves with single vein and pointed tips. Flowers 2-3mm in golden clusters, July-Aug. Fresh leaves smell of newly-mown hay and were once used for bedding, hence the common name. Not to be confused with crosswort.

Crosswort *Cruciata laevipes*

Hairy perennial to 60cm. Pale green, 3-veined leaves in whorls around stem. Flowers pale yellow, 2-3mm, in clusters at base of leaves, April-June. Common along the lanes here. Not to be confused with lady's bedstraw.

Figwort family *Scrophulariaceae*

Great mullein *Verbascum thapsus*

Sturdy biennial, appearing woolly as covered in white down, with unbranched main stem to 2m. Leaves very woolly, growing up against the stem. Flowers 15-30mm with 5 petals, 5 stamens, 2 of which are woolly, 3 hairless, June-Aug. In Westerdale this is probably a garden escape. In medieval times this plant was also known as the candlewick plant as the main stem was soaked in wax or tallow and used for light.

Dead-nettle family *Lamiaceae*

Yellow archangel
Lamiastrum galeobdolon ssp *argentatum*

Aka yellow dead-nettle and weasel snout. Erect, sparsely hairy, herbaceous perennial to 60cm. Leaves stalked and toothed with conspicuous white blotches. Flowers with upper hooded lip and 3-lobed lower lip, in dense whorls in leaf axils, corolla tube longer than calyx, May-June. This plant is naturalised in several local gardens.

Monkeyflower family *Phrymaceae*

Musk *Mimulus moschatus*

Perennial with leafy runners. Whole plant with sticky hairs. Leaves opposite, pale green with broad teeth and short stalks. Flowers pale yellow with *no red markings*, 10-20mm, June-Sept. Found growing along the river bank. No longer scented in spite of its common name.

Broomrape family *Orobanchaceae*

Common cow-wheat *Melampyrum pratense*

Semi-parasitic, hairless low growing annual found on moorland. Leaves in pairs, long and narrow with pointed tips. Flowers also in pairs with leaf-like bracts, 10-18mm, with 2 lips, the lower longer and flat with 3 lobes, May-Sept.

Yellow-rattle *Rhinanthus minor*

Aka hay rattle due to the noise made by the ripe fruits rattling in the wind within the remaining calyx. Semi-parasitic annual to 50cm usually found growing in hay meadows. Toothed leaves growing in opposite pairs along stem. Flowers 12-15mm, with fused sepals forming a swollen calyx; upper yellow lip tipped with purple, lower lip down turned, May-Sept.

Daisy family *Asteraceae*

Dandelions *Taraxacum* spp

An invasive garden weed with tenacious tap root, common on road sides. Low growing perennial with leaves in basal rosette. Hollow stems to 20cm with milky latex. Flowers 15-75mm, consist of yellow ray florets, outer ones often reddish below. Fruits enclosed in the familiar dandelion 'clock'.

Dandelions are known as a critical genus; 248 microspecies have been recognised in the British Isles but these are very difficult to differentiate. The following have been identified in Westerdale:[1]

Taraxacum acroglossum	*T. marklundii*
T. ancistrolobum	*T. ochrochlorum*
T. atactum	*T. pallidipes*
T. cordatum	*T. pannucium*
T. ekmanii	*T. pannulatiforme*
T. excertiforme	*T. piceatum*
T. fulviforme	*T. proximiforme*
T. hamatulum	*T. pseudohamatum*
T. hamatum	*T. sahlinianum*
T. lacerifolium	*T. sellandii*
T. lacistophyllum	*T. subcyanolepis*
T. landmarkii	*T. subhumatum*
T. laticordatum	*T. undulatiflorum*
T. lingulatum	

Coltsfoot *Tussilago farfara*

Early flowering perennial. Stems to 15cm with fleshy scales. Heart-shaped leaves appear much later than flowers. Flowers 15-35mm, solitary with disc and ray florets in flattish head, Feb-April. Fruit a conspicuous 'clock'. Aka as coughweed or coughwort as once used as a cough remedy.

1. I am very grateful to Vincent Jones, BSBI recorder for vc62, who in turn acknowledges the help of Professor John Richards in determining these species.

Groundsel *Senecio vulgaris*

Common annual to 30cm. Leaves narrow with ragged-looking uneven lobes, paler beneath. Flowers rayless, 4-5mm, held inside a tube of black-tipped bracts, Jan-Dec.

Common ragwort *Senecio jacobaea*

Hairless, biennial 30-100cm, branched at the top. Leaves ragged looking as unevenly lobed, terminal lobe short and *blunt*. Flowers 15-25mm, in flat-topped clusters, outer bracts few, *much shorter* than dark-tipped inner ones, June-Nov. Food plant of the caterpillars of the Cinnabar moth but much reduced due to eradication as poisonous to livestock especially horses.

Nipplewort *Lapsana communis*

Slender annual to 1m preferring partial shade. Upper leaves narrow and pointed, lower leaves with large teeth. Flowers pale yellow, 15-20mm in loose clusters, with short outer bracts, June-Oct.

Cat's-ear *Hypochaeris radicata*

Perennial characterised by scale-like bracts growing up leafless stem to 60 cm, only *slightly swollen* under the flowers. Leaves, with rounded lobes, in basal rosette. Flowers solitary, 25-40mm, outer florets grey beneath, May-Oct. Use hand lens to look for chaffy scales among florets. Fruits the familiar 'clock'. Found in similar habitats but not to be confused with autumn hawkbit.

Cat's-ear

Autumn hawkbit

Autumn hawkbit *Scorzoneroides autumnalis*

Variable perennial to 60cm, stem *swollen* below flowers, bracts only towards top of stem. Leaves very variable. Flowers only 12-35mm, in loose clusters, outer florets usually reddish beneath, *no* chaffy scales among florets. Fruits not beaked. Not to be confused with cat's-ear *qv*.

Hawkweed *Hieracium sabaudum forma sabaudum*

Hawkweeds are known as a critical genus as they are difficult to distinguish. Perennials with dandelion-like flower heads. Only one species found in Westerdale.[2] It has 40-50 stem leaves, stem covered in dense white hairs. Hawkweeds were so named because it was believed that hawks used the plant to improve their eyesight!

Mouse-ear hawkweed
Pilosella officinarum ssp *officinarum*

Softly hairy, low growing perennial to 30cm. Leaves rounded with soft white hairs above, white felted below. Flowers solitary, 20-30mm, lemon-yellow with outer florets reddish beneath, May-Aug. Found in short calcareous grassland.

Smooth hawk's-beard *Crepis capillaris*

Much branched annual, sometimes biennial, to 75cm. Leaves clasping the stem. Flowers 10-13mm, on slender stalks, outer florets usually tinged red beneath, June-Sept but often flowering later.

2. Thanks to Vincent Jones for this identification.

Pineappleweed *Matricaria discoidea*

Formerly *Matricaria matricarioides*. Low growing annual to 35cm smelling strongly of pineapple when crushed. Prefers well-trodden places, common by paths and field edges, often in gateways. Leaves much divided, soft and feathery. Flowers 5-10mm, disc florets only in a yellow/green domed head sitting in a cup of green bracts, May-Nov.

Smooth sow-thistle *Sonchus oleraceus*

Hairless annual, sometimes biennial to 2m, with milky latex. Leaves *dull*, relatively smooth with *pointed* auricles. Flowers pale yellow, 20-25mm, in clusters, April-Nov. Seeds held within the familiar 'clock'. Not to be confused with prickly sow-thistle.

Prickly sow-thistle *Sonchus asper*

Aka rough sow-thistle. Perennial to 2m. Differentiated from smooth sow-thistle by having *shiny*, *prickly* leaves with *rounded* auricles, June-Oct.

Corn sow-thistle *Sonchus arvensis*

Aka perennial sow-thistle. Robust, creeping perennial to 2m with milky latex and bristly upper stem. Leaves shiny green, long and toothed with long pointed lobes and rounded auricles. Flowers bright yellow, 40-50mm, in open clusters held within dark green bracts covered in glandular yellow hairs (use hand lens to view), July-Sept.

Yellow chamomile *Anthemis tinctoria*

Bg 2014. Erect, hairy biennial or short-lived perennial to 60cm. Leaves pinnate, deeply dissected. Flowers bright yellow, 25-40mm, July-Oct.

Fox-and-cubs *Pilosella aurantiaca*

Aka orange hawkweed. Unmistakable perennial to 40cm densely covered in hairs. Leaves lanceolate in basal rosette with very few along the stem. Flowers in close clusters, 13-15mm, with one usually more open than others, hence common name, June-Sept.

MONOCOTYLEDONS

Daffodil family *Amaryllidaceae*

Wild daffodil *Narcissus pseudonarcissus*

Known by several other names including daffydowndilly. Familiar plant to 35cm. Flowers with slightly darker yellow trumpet-like corona, March-April. Our only native narcissus, usually found growing in river-side woodland. Neighbouring Farndale is famous for its daffodils but Westerdale also has its own show. However, the yellow ribbon of flowers along the village street consists of planted, cultivated varieties.

Daffydowndilly is coming to town,
In a yellow petticoat and a green gown.

Bog asphodel family *Nartheciaceae*

Bog asphodel *Narthecium ossifragum*

Upright plant to 45cm. Leaves *flattened*, iris-like in basal tuft. Flowers star-like with 6 deep yellow tepals, often tinged with orange, 10-16mm, anthers orange, July-Aug. Fruiting spike deep orange. Found in bogs, peaty heaths and on moorland.

Red, pink and purple flowers

DICOTYLEDONS

Poppy family *Papaveraceae*

Common poppy *Papaver rhoeas*

A familiar arable weed. Annual to 70cm, stems with spreading hairs. Leaves divided and toothed, with coarse hairs. Flowers short-lived, solitary, 5-10cm with 2 sepals which soon fall and 4 scarlet petals blackened at base, June-Oct. Fruit a smooth flat-topped capsule releasing seeds like a pepper pot. Poppy seeds are extremely long-lived and can germinate long after falling once ground is disturbed, rarer here now there is very little arable land in Westerdale.

Opium poppy *Papaver somniferum*

Aka breadseed poppy. Bg 2014. Greyish, largely hairless annual to 120cm. Leaves grey green, coarsely toothed, slightly clasping stems. Flowers 10-18cm, white, mauve or red with darker centres, June-Oct. Fruit a rounded pepper-pot style capsule, sometimes dried for flower arrangements. In some countries certain varieties of this plant are cultivated for their opium-yielding latex, used in the production of morphine and codeine. The seeds are also used in bread making, hence the alternative common name.

Oriental poppy *Papaver orientale*

Sturdy perennial looking like an overgrown common poppy with larger, longer-lived flowers. Leaves hairy, divided and toothed. Single specimen has been seen flowering along the lane to Castleton for several decades.[1]

---

1. With thanks to the late Francesca Garforth for this information.

Common fumitory *Fumaria officinalis*

Delicate-looking, low growing annual giving the ground a smoky appearance when abundant, hence *Fumaria* from the French word for smoke. Leaves grey-green, much divided. Flowers 6-8mm, pink with darker tips, tubular and spurred with 2 lips, April-Oct. Fruits round. This is an unlikely looking member of the poppy family but recent DNA analysis has shown familial similarities.

White ramping fumitory *Fumaria capreolata*

Similar to above species but flowers 10-13mm, creamy white, often tinged pink with darker tips, May-Oct.

Buttercup family *Ranunculaceae*

Columbine *Aquilegia vulgaris*

Aka granny's bonnets. Hairless perennial to 1m. Leaves with 3 lobes, hairy above. Flowers bluish purple sometimes paler, 5 sepals, with nectar-carrying spurs, and 5 petals. Strictly a garden escape rather than a wild flower here. Botanical name derived from *aquila* for eagle, flowers said to resemble an eagle's claw. Common name derived from *columba* for dove, flowers said to resemble five doves clustered together.

Pea family *Fabaceae*

Red clover *Trifolium pratense*

Perennial with solid stems to 70cm; a common wayside flower. Trefoil leaves, stalked below, un-stalked above, leaflets toothed with characteristic white markings above. Stipules narrow with bristly tips. Flowers pinkish purple, rather than truly red, in rounded head 20-40mm, May-Nov. Pods egg-shaped. First cultivated in England in 1645, an important crop for enriching the land.

Bitter vetchling *Lathyrus linifolius*

Aka bitter vetch although this is confusing as it has winged stems therefore strictly not a vetch. Erect perennial to 40cm. Leaves with 2-4 narrow leaflets, no tendril just a point. Flowers reddish purple fading to blue, 2-6 on long-stalked head, April-July. Pods reddish brown, 25-45mm.

Bush vetch *Vicia sepium*

Scrambling perennial to 60cm. Leaves with 5-8 pairs of leaflets and branching tendrils. Flowers dull purple fading to blue, 12-15mm, 2-6 on short-stalk head, April-Nov. Pods hairless, 20-35mm, blackening as they ripen. A creamy yellow form of this species, sometimes known as a sport, has also been recorded in Westerdale; see under yellow flowers.

Common vetch *Vicia sativa* ssp *nigra*

Variable scrambling annual. Leaves with 3-8 pairs of leaflets, upper ones slightly narrower, ending in branched tendrils. Flowers 10-25mm, purple with standard paler than wings, usually in pairs, occasionally solitary, May-Sept. Pods 28-70mm, smooth and hairless, black or brown. In spite of its common name this is now a rare plant.

Tufted vetch *Vicia cracca*

Scrambling perennial to 2m, unmistakable when covering areas of hedgerow. Leaves with 8-12 pairs of leaflets. Flowers 8-12 mm, deep bluish purple growing along one side of the flower stalk, June-Aug. Pods hairless, brown, 10-25mm.

Wood-sorrel family *Oxalidaceae*

Pink oxalis *Oxalis articulata*

Aka pink sorrel. Perennial to 35cm. Leaves shamrock-like sometimes folded back on themselves with orange spots beneath. Flowers 10-15mm, with 5 usually deep pink petals, May-Sept. Garden escape.

Violet family *Violaceae*

Common dog violet *Viola riviniana*

Low growing perennial distinguished from other violets by its *pointed* sepals and more or less hairless heart-shaped leaves which are as broad as long. Flowers 12-18mm, zygomorphic with stout, usually cream-coloured spur and 5 mauve or bluish petals, lower petal with darker veining, March-May.

Marsh violet *Viola palustris*

Identified by *rounded* leaves with heart-shaped base, stems to 10cm. Flowers 10-15mm, pale lilac with darker veins, short spur, April-July. Found on marshes and wet heaths on acid ground.

Field pansy *Viola arvensis*

Low growing, much branched annual. Stipules toothed and leaf-like. Flowers small, familiar pansy form with *petals shorter than sepals,* sepals showing between the petals, April-Oct. Can be varying shades of yellow or mauve. See also under section on yellow flowers.

Crane's-bill family *Geraniaceae*

Dove's foot crane's-bill *Geranium molle*

Sprawling hairy annual to 40cm. Leaves rounded with 7-9 deeply cut lobes. Flowers 6-10mm with 5 pinkish purple notched petals, April-Sept. Fruits hairless, usually ridged.

Cut-leaved crane's-bill *Geranium dissectum*

Sprawling annual to 60cm. Leaves deeply cleft, nearly to base, with very narrow lobes. Flowers 8-10mm, deep pink petals with shallow notch at tip, May-Sept. Fruits downy.

Meadow crane's-bill *Geranium pratense*

Handsome perennial with reddish stems to 1m. Leaves with 7-9 deeply cut lobes. Flowers 25-30mm, growing in pairs, with 5 un-notched violet-blue petals, June-Sept. Fruit stalk bending down when ripe.

Herb Robert *Geranium robertianum*

Hairy annual to 50cm. Leaves with 3-5 lobes. Flowers 14-18mm, with orange pollen and 5 rounded, deep pink petals, April-Nov. Very common, found in a range of habitats. Formerly used for staunching wounds.

Willowherb family *Onagraceae*

Rosebay *Chamerion angustifolium*

Formerly rosebay willowherb (*Epilobium angustifolium*). Aka French willow. Conspicuous perennial to 1.5m. Leaves lanceolate. Flowers 20-30mm, with narrow reddish sepals and 4 unequal petals, June-Sept. Pods narrow, splitting longitudinally to release seeds with long plumes of silky hairs. Aka fireweed as it colonises an area after burning; often seen on bombed areas during and after World War II.

American willowherb *Epilobium ciliatum*

Fast-spreading, stems usually reddish. Leaves lanceolate, toothed. Flowers 8-10mm, pale pink with gaps between petals, stigma club-shaped, June-Aug. Pods short. Introduced to the UK in 1891, now well established.

© Ivan Sykes

Broad-leaved willowherb *Epilobium montanum*

Rounded stems. Leaves broad, toothed. Flowers 12-15mm, purple-pink, petals deeply notched, stigma cross-shaped, June-Aug. Prefers shade.

Great willowherb *Epilobium hirsutum*

Aka codlins and cream. Unmistakable, to 1.8m. Whole plant softly hairy. Leaves unstalked, lanceolate. Flowers 15-23mm, purple-pink, stigma cross-shaped, July-Sept.

Hoary willowherb *Epilobium parviflorum*

Looks like a miniature great willowherb, to 75cm. Leaves somewhat pointed. Flowers only 7-12mm, with deeply notched petals and cross-shaped stigma, July-Sept. Usually prefers dry locations but occasionally found in damp conditions.

© Ivan Sykes

Marsh willowherb *Epilobium palustre*

Slender plant with smooth, round stem to 60cm. Leaves sessile, narrow, lanceolate. Flowers pale pink, sometimes mauve or white, 8-12mm, with club-shaped stigmas, June-Aug. Found in wet acid soil often on moorland.

Short-fruited willowherb *Epilobium obscurum*

Leaves pale green, sessile. Flowers 7-9mm, sepals with glandular hairs, petals rose pink, July-Aug. Fruits relatively short, 4-6cm.

Willowherb hybrid

Epilobium parviflorum x *E obscurum* = *E* x *dacicum*

Mallow family *Malvaceae*

Common mallow *Malva sylvestris*

Bushy perennial to 1m. Leaves crinkly and toothed with dark spot at base. Flowers 3-4cm, deep pink with darker veins, 5 notched petals, June-Sept. Fruit a round flat nutlet looking like a small cheese hence aka cheesecakes or bread and cheese. Introduced to the UK from southern Europe, now well established.

Musk mallow *Malva moschata*

Attractive perennial with hairy stems to 80cm. Leaves deeply cleft with a feathery appearance. Flowers 3-6cm, pale pink with darker veins, June-Aug. Naturalised in several local gardens, possibly introduced by the Knights Templar as this was used as a medicinal plant in medieval times.

Cabbage family *Brassicaceae*

Dame's violet *Hesperis matronalis*

Aka sweet rocket and dame's gillyflower. Sturdy perennial to 1m. Leaves *lanceolate* and toothed. Flowers 15-20mm, very fragrant, with four petals, white or varying shades of lilac, May-Aug. Fruit a long cylindrical pod. The dame refers to Damascus; *Hesperis* is from the Greek for evening when the scent is most pronounced. Not to be confused with honesty. See also under section on white flowers.

Honesty *Lunaria annua*

Biennial to 1m. Leaves toothed, *heart-shaped*. Flowers 28-31mm, purple or white, April-June. Fruits round flattened pods, green at first then like silver pennies, used for decoration. Not to be confused with dame's violet.

Lady's smock *Cardamine pratensis*

Aka milkmaids and cuckoo flowers as in flower when the cuckoo arrives. Unbranched perennial to 60cm. Lower leaves in basal rosette, stem leaves with narrow leaflets. Flowers 10-18mm, usually pale mauve,

rarely white, anthers yellow, April-June. Seed pods held upright. Prefers damp meadows or stream sides. Lady's smock was once sold as meadow bittercress and used in salads, made famous by Shakespeare's lines:

When daisies pied and violets blue
And lady-smock all silver-white
And cuckoo buds of yellow hue
Do paint the meadows with delight.

Dock family *Polygonaceae*

Knotgrass *Polygonum aviculare*

Sprawling or erect hairless annual to 1m. Leaves oval with those on main stem much longer than those on branches. Flowers small in clusters of 2 or 3 together with white or pink *tepals*, June-Nov. Flowers partly enclosed in a papery sheath giving a knotted appearance, hence common name. Often found in field gateways.

Equal-leaved knotgrass *Polygonum arenastrum*

Much-branched, mat-forming annual to 30cm. Similar to knotgrass but leaves *all the same size and overlapping*. Flowers with greenish white *tepals*, July-Nov. Found along well-trodden paths and gateways. See also under section on green plants.

Redshank *Persicaria maculosa*

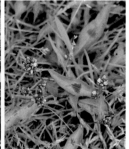

Aka redleg, formerly *Polygonum persicaria*. Erect annual to 80cm with red stems swollen at nodes. Leaves with characteristic dark marking above, often whitish beneath. Flowers small and pink, overlapping in rough spikes, June-Sept. Prefers damp muddy locations, usually found in arable fields.

Pink family *Caryophyllaceae*

Red campion *Silene dioica*

Perennial to 1m. Whole plant softly hairy. Leaves pointed ovals, without petioles. Tubular calyx of *brownish red* hairy sepals. Flowers 18-25mm, rosy pink, occasionally white, with 5 cleft petals; male and female on separate plants, March-Nov. Fruit a capsule with 10 rolled back teeth. See also white campion.

Campion hybrid *Silene x hampeana*

A cross between red and white campion with paler calyx and pinkish petals.

Ragged robin *Silene flos-cuculi*

Formerly *Lychnis flos-cuculi*. Easily identified perennial to 75cm. Leaves in opposite pairs, narrow and pointed. Flowers 3-4cm on long stalks with 5 *deeply cleft* petals giving them a ragged appearance, styles and stamens in same flowers, May-July. Fruits with 5 teeth. Prefers damp meadowland.

Corncockle *Agrostemma githago*

Bg 2014. Handsome, hairy annual to 1m. Leaves greyish green, lance-shaped. Flowers deep pink, 3-5cm, with 5 calyx teeth longer than the 5 petals, June-Aug. Corncockle has now been eradicated from the wild as it is poisonous to grain but is often sown in mixes of wild flower seeds as here.

Blinks family *Montiaceae*

Pink purslane *Claytonia sibirica*

Annual to 40cm. Lower leaves stalked. Flowers usually pink, 16-20mm, with 5 notched petals growing in stalked clusters above opposite pairs of leaves, April-July. Prefers damp shady places. Introduced from western United States of America in the 1760s.

Balsam family *Balsaminaceae*

Himalayan balsam *Impatiens glandulifera*

Aka Indian balsam and policemen's helmets. Hairless annual with reddish stems to 2m. Leaves in whorls, toothed. Flowers 25-40mm, fragrant, pinkish purple, sometimes white, with thin bent spur. An aggressive coloniser of stream banks. Measures have been taken to eradicate this in Westerdale; introduced to the UK in 1835 it has become very invasive.

Primrose family *Primulaceae*

Bog pimpernel *Anagallis tenella*

Slender, creeping, evergreen perennial to 15cm. Stems rooting at nodes. Leaves rounded and very small, opposite and entire, looking like beads on a string. Flowers pink on slender stalks much longer than leaves. Petals twice as long as sepals, June-Aug. Found on the margins of acid pools, in marshes and on moorland.

Heath family *Ericaceae*

Cross-leaved heath *Erica tetralix*

Greyish undershrub to 70cm. Leaves in whorls of 4 along stem, glandular hairs on sepals and leaves. Flowers rose-pink, 5-9mm in clustered heads, June-Oct. Found on *damp* moorland.

Bell heather *Erica cinerea*

Hairless undershrub to 60cm. Leaves dark green in whorls of 3, with in-rolled edges covering underside. Flowers reddish purple, 4-6mm, in spikes or clustered heads, June-Sept. The brightest coloured of the heaths, found on *drier* moorland.

Heather *Calluna vulgaris*

Aka ling. Ground covering undershrub to 60cm. Leaves linear, in opposite rows along stem, sometimes downy. Flowers in spikes, pinkish mauve, 3-4mm with 4 fused petals, July-Sept. Occasionally a white flowered plant can be found and is considered to be 'lucky heather'. Formerly used for thatching; the houses here would once have been thatched with ling. Also used for fuel. Nineteenth century entries in the logbooks of Castleton School record boys being sent out to collect ling for the stove; it is more than likely that this also happened at Westerdale.

Bilberry *Vaccinium myrtillus*

Dwarf deciduous shrub to 30cm. Twigs green, conspicuously ridged. Leaves bright green. Flowers pink, bell-like 4-6mm, April-June. Fruits spherical, black with white bloom. Familiar on moorland, fruit used for pies. See also under section on green plants.

Cowberry *Vaccinium vitis-idaea*

Straggly sub-shrub to 20cm, twigs downy when young. Leaves *evergreen*, oval, rather leathery, margins entire, dark green above, paler below. Flowers pale pink, bell-shaped, 5-6mm, May-June. Fruits shiny red berries. Towards the south-eastern limit of its range. See also under section on green plants.

Borage family *Boraginaceae*

Russian comfrey *Symphytum* x *uplandicum*

Hairy perennial with bristly stems to 1.5m. Leaves pointed ovals, basal leaves with long stalks, upper leaves only slightly running down the leaf stalks. Flowers with 5 fused petals, varying shades of purple curled into a dense cyme. Fruit a smooth nutlet. Hybrid between common and rough comfrey, introduced from eastern Europe in 1870 as a fodder plant. Comfreys are aka knitbone as once used to heal broken limbs. The word 'comfrey' is derived from con *firma* meaning made firm; *Symphytum* from the Greek meaning 'to unite'. Comfrey has been shown to contain a number of chemicals such as allantoin and rosmarinic acid both of which aid the healing process.

Speedwell family *Veronicaceae*

The following two species are also listed in the section on blue flowers in order to be seen alongside other speedwells.

Heath speedwell *Veronica officinalis*

Mat-forming hairy perennial to 40cm. Stems creeping, hairy all round. Leaves oval, toothed, narrowed to short stalks. Flowers mauve, 6-9mm, on stalks longer than leaf-like bracts at their base, May-Aug. Fruits longer than broad.

Ivy-leaved speedwell *Veronica hederifolia* ssp *lucorum*

Prostrate hairy annual to 50cm. Leaves pale green, palmately lobed. Flowers 4-6mm, pale lilac March-Aug. Fruits rounded, hairless. A weed of disturbed ground.

Dead-nettle family *Lamiaceae*

Apple mint *Mentha* x *villosa* var. *alopecuroides*

Aka garden apple mint. Hybrid between round-leaved and spear mint, to 90cm. Leaves rounded and softly hairy. Flowers small, mauve with 4 protruding stamens and 4 more or less equal petals growing in branched spike, Aug-Sept. Characteristic minty/apple scent.

Round-leaved mint *Mentha suaveolens*

Perennial to 90cm. Leaves rounded and wrinkled with blunt teeth and characteristic scent. Flowers pinkish mauve 2-3mm, in a branched spike, Aug-Sept.

Spear mint *Mentha spicata*

Strongly aromatic branched perennial to 90cm, stems reddish. Leaves sessile, lanceolate. Flowers in *terminal spike*, Aug-Sept. Prefers damp locations. Introduced by the Romans, the herb cultivated for mint sauce. Mints have been valued since ancient times. The Bible speaks of the Pharisees collecting tithes in mint, among other herbs. It was also used as a strewing herb. Writing in 1597, the herbalist Gerard tells us that 'they use it to strew in places of recreation, pleasure and repose where feasts and banquets are made.'

Betony *Betonica officinalis*

Aka bishop's wort. Slightly hairy perennial to 75cm. Leaves with very short stalks and rounded teeth, mostly in basal rosette with few in pairs along stem. Flowers 12-18mm, reddish purple, June-Oct. This plant was highly valued throughout the medieval period as a cure-all; the Emperor Augustus (63BC – AD14) claimed that betony would cure 47 different illnesses. Modern analysis has shown that it is not a panacea but it is still used in herbal medicine as a remedy for headaches. The plant contains several alkaloids and tannins.

Bifid hemp-nettle *Galeopsis bifida*

Easily missed annual with bristly stems to 1m. Leaves well toothed, nettle-like. Flowers deep pink, with darker markings on *notched* lower lip, 13-20mm, July-Sept. Not to be confused with common hemp-nettle *qv*.

Hedge woundwort *Stachys sylvatica*

Roughly hairy perennial with both erect and creeping stems to 1m. Whole plant rather pungent. Leaves toothed, heart-shaped, lower stalked, upper sessile. Flowers 13-18mm, growing in whorls around stem, 5 sepal teeth, upper lip hooded with 4 stamens, lower lip with 3 lobes, deep beetroot-red with white blotches, June-Oct. As its common name suggests this was used as a healing plant. Modern chemical analysis has shown that it includes both antiseptic and anaesthetic properties.

Ground-ivy *Glechoma hederacea*

Perennial to 30cm with long rooting runners to 1m. Leaves on long stalks, kidney-shaped with blunt teeth. Flowers 15-20mm, bluish purple, March-June. Aka alehoof as used to flavour ale before hops were introduced to England.

Red dead-nettle *Lamium purpureum*

Sprawling annual to 40cm. Leaves heart-shaped with short rounded teeth, all stalked. Flowers 10-18mm, pinkish purple, Jan-Dec. A familiar weed of cultivation.

Self-heal *Prunella vulgaris*

Creeping downy perennial to 30cm completely without scent. Leaves pointed ovals with wavy margins rather than teeth. Flowers 10-15mm, bluish violet, with purple sepals, growing together at top of flower stalk, June-Oct. Can become a nuisance in the garden lawn.

Figwort family *Scrophulariaceae*

Common figwort *Scrophularia nodosa*

Hairless perennial with *square stems* to 1m. Oval leaves pointed and toothed. Flowers 7-10mm, purple-brown, 5 stamens, 1 without an anther (staminode), sepals with pale margins, June-Aug. A plant difficult to classify by colour.

Speedwell family *Veronicaceae*

Foxglove *Digitalis purpurea*

Familiar wayside biennial to 2m. Leaves wrinkled with downy hairs, lower leaves in basal rosette. Flowers deep pink, 40-55mm, like thimbles or the finger ends of a glove, up to 80 in a tall unbranched spike, June-Sept. Yields the drug *digitalis* and remains an important medicinal plant.

Ivy-leaved toadflax *Cymbalaria muralis*

Trailing, hairless perennial to 60cm often growing in stone walls. Leaves not dissimilar to ivy. Flowers 9-15mm, mauve with yellow splash on lower lip, on long slender stalks. Flowers grow out towards the light while the fruits grow away from it hence colonising walls. Introduced in the seventeenth century and now well established.

Daisy family *Asteraceae*

Black knapweed *Centaurea nigra*

Aka common knapweed or hardheads. Perennial with stiff, ridged stems to 1m, stem swollen below flower head. Leaves lanceolate, lower leaves toothed. Hard round receptacle covered in brown, pale edged bracts. Flowers consist of purple florets in head 2-4cm, June-Sept.

Wood burdock *Arctium nemorosum*

Robust branched biennial to 2m. Leaves large broad ovals, paler beneath. Flowers on very short stalks, in purple brush-like head with bracts ending in hooked bristles which remain in fruit and attach themselves to clothing and animal fur, July-Sept. *Arctium* sp inspired the development of Velcro. In some parts of the country children now call these Velcro plants – nature imitating art, or art imitating nature?

Creeping thistle *Cirsium arvense*

Common perennial to 2m with creeping rootstock. Leaves spiny but *spineless* stem. Flowers 10-20mm, pale mauve, occasionally white, very fragrant with purplish green bracts below, in terminal cluster, June-Oct. Found on rough ground and pasture land.

Marsh thistle *Cirsium palustre*

Erect biennial with spiny-winged stems to 2m. Basal leaf rosette tinged purple making it unmistakable. Leaves narrow with purple-tipped spines. Flowers in tightly packed head, 10-15mm, rich purple with purple-tipped bracts, June-Oct. Fruits with feathery down.

Spear thistle *Cirsium vulgare*

Unmistakable stout biennial with spiny-winged stems to 1.5m. Leaves lobed and spiny. Flowers usually solitary, 20-40mm, with yellow-tipped green bracts, July-Sept. Fruits with pappus of feathery hairs.

Musk thistle *Carduus nutans*

Grey cottony biennial with winged stems to 1m. Leaves lobed and spiny. Bracts purple-tipped, conspicuously turned back from flowers. Flowers 20-60mm, deep purple, fragrant, usually solitary with characteristic nodding habit, June-Sept.

Winter heliotrope *Petasites fragrans*

Patch-forming perennial. Leaves rounded, remaining throughout the year. Flower stalks hollow and hairy, to 30cm. Flowers fragrant, purple to pale lilac in spikes of several blooms each looking like a shaving brush, Dec-March. Does not flower every year. Introduced to the UK from North Africa in 1806 now naturalised in many parts of the country. Not to be confused with butterbur (*Petasite hybridus*), which is not found in Westerdale.

Teasel family *Dipsacaceae*

Devil's-bit scabious *Succisa pratensis*

Downy perennial to 1m. Roots are very short, said to have been bitten off in a devilish plot! Leaves long and thin often with purple blotches, few along stem, sometimes toothed. Flowers bluish purple with green bracts of varying lengths, in rounded head 15-25mm, with protruding pink or purple anthers, June-Oct.

Field scabious *Knautia arvensis*

Aka lady's pincushion. Sturdy, hairy perennial to 1m. Some leaves lobed, others toothed, basal leaves overwintering. Sepal-like bracts in two uneven rows. Flowers bluish mauve in flat head, 15-30mm, outer flowers larger than inner all with 4 unequal petals, protruding stamens and pink anthers looking like pins in a pin cushion, June-Oct.

Wild teasel *Dipsacus fullonum*

Bg 2014. Unmistakable biennial with spiny stems to 3m. Leaves prickly, stem leaves narrower than basal leaves, cupped at base and catching rain water. Conical flower head 4-8cm surrounded by upward pointing spines. Flowers mauve, those around centre opening first, July-Sept. Dead flower heads persist all winter, often used in flower arrangements. Formerly used in fulling mills to tease out wool before spinning or to raise the nap or pile on fabric, still used in some instances.

MONOCOTYLEDONS

Orchid family *Orchidaceae*

Four species of orchid have been recorded in Westerdale. They are tricky to identify and are known to readily hybridise to confuse the unwary. Two of the species were found in an area that has probably never been ploughed and is known to have been meadowland in medieval times. Orchids do not flower every year and can lie dormant for decades.

Common spotted orchid *Dactylorhiza fuschii*

Very variable perennial with solid stem to 50cm. Leaves narrow with parallel veins, usually with dark *transverse* spots. Flowers in pointed spike varying from mauve to deep purple, with darker blotches. Labellum with three slightly wavy lobes marked with darker lines, middle lobe *equal to or slightly longer than* lateral lobes, long spur, June-Aug. Found in calcareous grassland. Seen in flower in 2017 and a second specimen, different location, in 2018.

Heath spotted orchid *Dactylorhiza maculata*

Similar to common spotted orchid but leaves with more circular spots and with a blunter flower spike. Labellum with narrow central tooth *shorter* than round lateral lobes, June-Aug. Found on moorland and in bogs on *acid* soil. Seen in flower in 2018.

Northern marsh orchid *Dactylorhiza purpurella*

Sturdy perennial to 25cm. Leaves stiffly spreading, usually unspotted. Flowers reddish purple with darker markings, in broad, flat-topped inflorescence. Flowers with stout spurs, labellum 7-9mm, diamond-shaped with a central tooth, bracts purplish, June-July. Seen in flower in 2018.

Southern marsh orchid *Dactylorhiza praetermissa*

Sturdy perennial to 50cm. Leaves dark green, usually unspotted. Flowers rose-purple, spur short and stout, labellum broad with small central tooth, sepals spreading, bracts and upper stem often purplish, June-July. Towards northern limits of its range so a very good find in Westerdale. Seen in flower in 2017.

Blue flowers

Milkwort family *Polygalaceae*

Heath milkwort *Polygala serpyllifolia*

Slender hairless perennial to 30cm. Leaves lanceolate, unstalked and fairly crowded along stem, lower leaves *opposite*. Flowers 5-6mm of unusual shape appearing to have 5 petals but with 3 outer sepals and 2 petal-like sepals folded out like wings over the 3 tiny fringed petals, May-Sept. Usually blue but sometimes white or mauve, see also under section on white flowers.

Borage family *Boraginaceae*

Borage *Borago officinalis*

Sturdy, hairy annual to 60cm. Leaves oval with wavy edges. Flowers readily recognised by their bright blue, reflexed petals surrounding a column of black stamens, May-Sept. Has in recent years been sown in the dale for honey production thus an escape of cultivation. At one time used medicinally. The flowers were floated in the stirrup-cups served to Crusaders as they left for Jerusalem.

Changing forget-me-not *Myosotis discolor*

Low growing annual to 25cm. Leaves hairy, oval, greyish green. Flowers 1-2mm, yellow on opening, changing to blue, May-Sept. Fruit a blackish nutlet.

Creeping forget-me-not *Myosotis secunda*

Creeping perennial to 70cm. Characterised by spreading hairs on lower stems. Flowers greyish blue, 6-8mm with long pedicels but very short styles and *slightly notched* petals. Found in acidic pools or runnels on moorland.

Field forget-me-not *Myosotis arvensis*

Low growing annual weed of cultivation to 40cm. Leaves oval, downy and unstalked. Flowers greyish blue, petals *shorter* than their tubes, 2-5mm, April-Oct. Fruit a blackish nutlet.

Wood forget-me-not *Myosotis sylvatica*

Perennial to 50cm. Leaves oval, hairy. Flowers flat, sky blue, 6-10mm with petals *much longer* than tubes, April-July. Fruit a dark brown, pointed nutlet. Often a garden escape.

Speedwell family *Veronicaceae*

Brooklime *Veronica beccabunga*

Hairless sprawling perennial to 60cm found in shallow pools and streams. Leaves oval with short stalks, bluntly toothed. Flowers deep blue, 5-7mm, May-Sept. Fruits rounded.

Common field speedwell *Veronica persica*

Sprawling hairy annual to 60cm. Leaves pale green, rounded and toothed, hairy below. Flowers 8-12mm, sky blue with darker veins, lower petal usually white, Jan-Dec. Fruit with two widely diverging lobes. Usually a weed of arable land so now found less frequently in Westerdale. First recorded in UK in 1825.

Germander speedwell *Veronica chamaedrys*

Aka birds' eyes. Common perennial to 50cm with two lines of hairs along reddish stems. Leaves hairy, bluntly toothed. Flowers bright blue with a white eye, April-July. Fruits broadly heart-shaped. Often seen as a weed of garden lawns.

Heath speedwell *Veronica officinalis*

Mat-forming hairy perennial to 40cm. Stems creeping, hairy all round. Leaves oval, toothed, narrowed to short stalks. Flowers mauve, 6-9mm, on stalks longer than leaf-like bracts at their base, May-Aug. Fruits longer than broad. Also listed in section on red, pink and purple flowers.

Ivy-leaved speedwell *Veronica hederifolia* ssp *lucorum*

Prostrate hairy annual to 50cm. Leaves pale green, palmately lobed. Flowers 4-6mm, pale lilac March-Aug. Fruits rounded, hairless. A weed of disturbed ground. Also listed in section on red, pink and purple flowers.

Thyme-leaved speedwell
Veronica serpyllifolia ssp *serpyllifolia*

Hairless, creeping perennial to 30cm. Leaves oval, shiny, untoothed. Flowers very pale with bluish violet veins, on stalks shorter than leaf-like bracts at their base, April-Oct. Fruits slightly broader than long.

Wall speedwell *Veronica arvensis*

Hairy annual to 20cm. Leaves dark green, oval, toothed. Flowers deep blue, only 2-3mm, often hidden by untoothed upper leaves, March-Oct. Fruits heart-shaped, about as long as broad.

Dead-nettle family *Lamiaceae*

Bugle *Ajuga reptans*

Leafy perennial to 30cm with long rooting runners, usually found in damp woodland. Characterised by stems hairy on two opposite sides. Leaves hairless, oval, often bronzed, lower leaves in a rosette. Flowers 14-17mm with 5 sepal teeth, growing in a leafy spike among purplish, leaf-like bracts, April-July.

Bellflower family *Campanulaceae*

Harebell *Campanula rotundifolia*

Aka Scottish bluebell. Slender, hairless perennial to 50cm. Basal leaves rounded, hence botanical name, stem leaves narrow, linear. Flowers 10-20mm, pale blue hanging bells on slender stalks, July-Sept. Just occasionally a white flower may be found.

Daisy family *Asteraceae*

Chicory *Cichorium intybus*

Aka succory. Stiff perennial to 1m. Leaves unstalked, lanceolate, lower leaves lobed. Flowers 25-40mm, bright blue, unstalked along stem. Our only native blue dandelion-like flower. Young shoots used in salads, root is ground and used as a coffee substitute.

Cornflower *Centaurea cyanus*

Bg 2014. Downy annual to 80cm. Upper leaves long and narrow covered in cottony hairs. Flowers 15-30mm, bright blue with spreading outer florets, June-Aug. Seed head the familiar 'clock' beloved of goldfinches. Once a common arable weed now eradicated by herbicides but found in wild flower seed mixes as here. Aka bluebottle as the petals were once pressed for making ink.

MONOCOTYLEDONS

Asparagus family *Asparagaceae*

English bluebell *Hyacinthoides non-scripta*

Bulbous perennial to 50cm carpeting woodland in spring. Leaves all basal, linear, hairless, shiny green. Flowers 14-20mm, azure blue, rarely white, in sets of up to 12 in one-sided spike drooping at tip. Individual bell-like flowers with 6 recurved tips and *cream* anthers, April-May. Bluebell bulbs contain starch, used in Elizabethan times to stiffen ruffs.

Bluebell hybrid *Hyacinthoides x massartiana*

This is a hybrid between English bluebell (*Hyacinthoides non-scripta*) and Spanish bluebell (*H. hispanica*) even though the Spanish bluebell is absent. More erect than English bluebell, leaves broader, flowers paler with *blue* anthers, April-May.

Green plants

The plants in this section have flowers that are either inconspicuous or have a very short flowering season. Some of them have been included in another colour section but are also entered here as they largely present as green specimens.

Saxifrage family *Saxifragaceae*

Opposite-leaved golden saxifrage
Chrysosplenium oppositifolium

Low creeping perennial with *square* stems to 15cm. Leaves growing in matted patches, rounded, bluntly toothed, on *opposite* sides of stem. Flowers 3-4mm, *without petals*, with yellowish-green sepals and bracts and bright yellow anthers, Feb-July. Found by stream-sides and other wet places. See also under section on yellow flowers.

Nettle family *Urticaceae*

Stinging nettle *Urtica dioica*

Familiar patch-forming perennial to 2m. Likes shady places, often found around human habitation where soil is rich in nitrogen. Leaves deeply toothed with coarse stinging hairs. Flowers tiny, greenish with yellow anthers in narrow catkins, male and female on separate plants, May-Sept. Well known as a pot herb, used to make soups and teas, but also an important textile plant as it produces a very strong fibre.

Nettles are sometimes visited by gall wasps which lay their eggs on the stem, leaves or flowers. The larvae then cause a pouch to develop, which can be seen on the surface of the plant. Nettles can also be attacked by the fungus *Puccinia urticata*, aka nettle rust.

Spurge family *Euphorbaceae*

Dog's mercury *Mercurialis perennis*

Unbranched, carpeting perennial to 40cm, an indicator of ancient woodland. Leaves opposite, dark green, lanceolate, toothed. Flowers without petals on erect spikes. Dioecious; male catkins with numerous yellow anthers, female with stalks that lengthen as fruits develop, Feb-May. Fruit a 2-celled hairy nut. It was the study of this plant that led botanists to confirm that plants reproduce sexually.

Petty spurge *Euphorbia peplus*

Hairless annual to 20cm often branching from the base. Leaves oval, untoothed with blunt tips. Flowerheads green, *without petals or sepals* but with slender crescent-shaped lobes, April-Nov. Fruits with wavy edges. Found along path edges.

Cabbage family *Brassicaceae*

Field penny-cress *Thlaspi arvense*

Hairless foetid annual to 60cm. Leaves yellowish, shiny and toothed, clasping stem with rounded lobes. Flowers white with yellow anthers, 4-6mm, May-Sept. Fruit a circular pod with broad wing, notched at top looking penny-like, hence common name. Most noticeable in fruit. An arable weed thus much less frequent now. See also under section on white flowers.

Dock family *Polygonaceae*

All docks are often called dockens in the north of England. They have thin papery sheaths, ochrea, at the base of the leaf stalk or petiole.

Broad-leaved dock *Rumex obtusifolius*

Well-known persistent perennial on robust stems to 1m. Leaves with heart-shaped bases and slightly wavy edges. Lower leaves stalked, upper leaves sessile. Flowers in whorls on upper stem, June-Oct. Fruit with one enlarged reddish wart.

Curled dock *Rumex crispus*

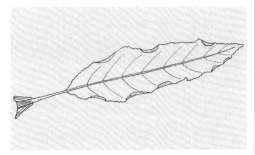

Perennial with branched stems to 1m. Leaves narrow with distinctive curled or crisped edges. Flowers in dense branched spikes, with triangular tepals, June-Oct. Fruit pale, untoothed with one large wart.

Dock hybrid *Rumex x pratensis*

Hybrid between broad-leaved and curled docks with broad but only slightly crisped leaves. The most common dock hybrid.

Wood dock *Rumex sanguineus*

Short-lived perennial with *upright* stems to 60cm; our only shade-loving dock. Leaves lanceolate, lower leaves oval and pointed. Flowers with oblong tepals, in spikes, leafy only on lower stalk, June-July. Fruit with round wart on one smooth-edged tepal.

Common sorrel *Rumex acetosa*

Unbranched perennial to 80cm. Leaves arrow-shaped with *backward pointing* basal lobes, upper leaves sessile and clasping stem. Flowers small, reddish, in compact leafless spikes, May-July. Fruit roundish with one tiny wart. At one time used for culinary and medicinal purposes.

Sheep's sorrel *Rumex acetosella*

Slender perennial to 20cm. Leaves narrow with basal lobes pointing *sideways or forwards*. Flowers in open spikes, April-July. Fruit *without* warts. When growing in patches gives a reddish tinge to areas of moorland.

Equal-leaved knotgrass *Polygonum arenastrum*

Much-branched, *mat-forming* annual to 30cm. Similar to knotgrass but leaves *all the same size and overlapping*. Flowers with greenish-white tepals, July-Nov. Found along well-trodden paths and in gateways.

Knotgrass *Polygonum aviculare*

Sprawling or erect, hairless annual to 1m. Leaves oval with those on main stem much longer than those on branches. Flowers small in clusters of 2 or 3 together with white or pink *tepals*, June-Nov. Flowers partly enclosed in a papery sheath giving a knotted appearance, hence common name. Often found in field gateways. See also under red, pink and purple flowers.

Pink family *Caryophyllaceae*

Procumbent pearlwort *Sagina procumbens*

Low growing *perennial* to 20cm, usually much shorter, with non-flowering, *basal rosette of leaves*. Flowers on slender stalks, with 4 greenish white petals *much shorter* than 4 blunt green sepals, April-Sept. Found on bare ground as well as in cracks in garden paths.

Annual pearlwort *Sagina apetala*

Well-branched pale green *annual* to 15cm, usually much shorter. Leaves narrow, linear, fused at base. Flowers tiny, greenish white, April-Aug. Sepals pointed and upright around fruit. Annual pearlwort differs from procumbent pearlwort in not having a central rosette of leaves.

Goosefoot family *Amaranthaceae*

Common orache *Atriplex patula*

Variable, mealy annual sprawling or erect to 1m often found by field edges. Leaves usually lanceolate, lower leaves more triangular narrowing into stalk. Flowers somewhat insignificant in slender spikes, July-Sept.

Fat hen *Chenopodium album*

Well-branched annual to 1.5m, stems sometimes tinged purple at leaf nodes. Leaves lanceolate to diamond-shaped, lower leaves mealy when immature. Flowers in leafy spikes, June-Oct. Found on disturbed ground. For many centuries, from the Bronze Age onwards, seeds were included in the diet. Seeds of fat hen were found in the stomach of the well-preserved Iron Age Tollund Man, found on the Jutland peninsular in 1950.

Good King Henry *Chenopodium bonus-henricus*

Perennial to 50cm. Stems mealy when young, reddening with age. Leaves broadly triangular with wavy margins, 10cm long and up to 8cm wide, mealy at first, becoming smooth and green. Flowers in erect, terminal pyramidal spike on leafless stalks. Flowers with 5 sepals, 5 stamens and 2-3 stigmas, May-Aug. Introduced here by the Romans but known to have been used throughout Europe since Neolithic times. In Germany this is known as Good Henry to distinguish it from mercury, which is known as Bad Henry as it is poisonous. The King in the English common name was added in Tudor times in honour of Henry VIII.

Fodder beet *Beta vulgaris* ssp *vulgaris*

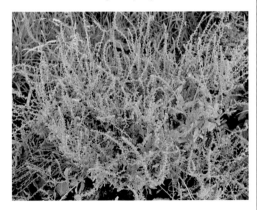

Aka root beet and mangelwurzel or mangold-wurzel. Annual herb with erect stems to 1.5m. Root much swollen, used for animal feed. A relic of cultivation.

Blinks family *Montiaceae*

Blinks *Montia fontana*

Very low growing, cushion forming, short-lived perennial, stems slightly reddish. Flowers tiny with 5 white petals in clusters of up to 3 on short stalks, April-Oct. Grows in damp places.

Heath family *Ericaceae*

Bilberry *Vaccinium myrtillus*

In other parts of the country aka blaeberry, whortleberry and huckleberry. Deciduous undershrub with hairless, green angled stems to 30cm. Leaves oval, finely toothed. Flowers deep pink, bell-shaped with 5 tiny teeth, usually hidden in pairs in leaf axils, April-June. Fruits the familiar edible bluish black berry with white bloom, July-Aug. Carpets areas of moorland with its bright green leaves. See also in section on red, pink and purple flowers.

Cowberry *Vaccinium vitis-idaea*

Straggly sub-shrub to 20cm, twigs downy when young. Leaves *evergreen*, oval, rather leathery, margins entire, dark green above, paler below. Flowers 5-6mm, bell-shaped, May-June. Fruits shiny red berries.

Crowberry *Empetrum nigrum*

Evergreen heather-like shrub to 45cm. Leaves smooth with turned back margins. Flowers *very small*, pink with 3 sepals and 3 petals, Jan-April. Fruit similar to a bilberry but much smaller and without the bloom. Found on moorland.

Bedstraw family *Rubiaceae*

Goosegrass *Galium aparine*

Aka sweethearts, cleavers and sitcky willie. Troublesome hedgerow weed resistant to many herbicides, often scrambling to 3m. Catches on animal fur or people's clothing due to many curved prickles. Leaves in whorls along the stem, wider towards tip, ending in a minute bristle. Flowers inconspicuous, 1-2mm, May-Sept. Fruits spherical, covered in hooked bristles. Lacemakers used to stick the fruits of goosegrass onto their pins to give them larger heads.

Plantain family *Plantaginaceae*

Greater plantain *Plantago major*

Aka rats' tails. Familiar weed of verge edges, field gates and other bare well-trodden places. Stout hairless perennial to 40cm. Leaves broadly oval often with wavy edges and prominent veins on underside. Flowers in long greenish spike on *unfurrowed* stalks, pale yellow with purple anthers fading to brown, June-Oct. Aka waybread, the *wæbrod* of the Old English Herbarium, an important healing plant throughout the Middle Ages and still used in herbal medicine today; the leaves contain tannins and astringent chemicals.

Ribwort plantain *Plantago lanceolata*

Another familiar wayside perennial to 50cm. Leaves lanceolate, slightly toothed with 3-5 prominent ribs on underside. Flowers in dense spikes, 2-4cm, blackish brown at first then light brown with pale yellow anthers, on *furrowed* stalks, April-Oct.

Water-starwort family *Callitrichaceae*

Common water-starwort *Callitriche stagnalis*

Aquatic annual or short-lived perennial. Submerged leaves oval, terrestrial leaves more rounded. Flowers tiny, *without* petals or sepals, male a single stamen, female a 4-celled ovary, May-Sepr. Fruits greyish with distinct wings. Found in muddy pools and ditches.

Ivy family *Araliaceae*

Ivy *Hedera helix*

Evergreen woody climber common on trees and walls, clinging with tiny roots, to 30m. Leaves very variable from the more familiar ivy-shape 5 lobes, shiny and leathery on non-flowering shoots, to dark green, purple-tinged ovals on older stems. Flowers 7-9mm, green with yellow anthers in erect umbel, Sept-Nov. Fruits dull black berries throughout the winter.

Pennywort family *Hydrocotylaceae*

Marsh pennywort *Hydrocotyle vulgaris*

Prostrate creeping perennial to 30cm found in bogs and other wet acidic places. Leaves rounded with shallow lobes, held on central stalks like parasols. Flowers reddish in bud, then greenish pink with yellow anthers, *tiny, 1mm*, difficult to find as hidden among leaves, June-Aug. Fruits tiny, flattened rounds.

MONOCOTYLEDONS

Arum family *Araceae*

Lords and ladies *Arum maculatum*

Aka wild arum, cuckoo pint, preacher in the pulpit and over 100 other common (sometimes rude!) names. A singular plant, to 25cm, with large arrow-shaped leaves sometimes with dark blotches, appearing from Feb. Flowers consist of pale green, leaf-like cowl, the spathe, enclosing the strongly-smelling purple spadix that attracts insects, which then pollinate the tiny enclosed flowers, April-June. Fruits **very poisonous** in a spike of orange-red berries. Aka starchwort as the roots yield a very effective starch used to stiffen Elizabethan and Jacobean ruffs.

Arrowgrass family *Juncaginaceae*

Marsh arrowgrass *Triglochin palustris*

In spite of its common name this is not a grass – and doesn't look particularly like an arrow! Difficult to find among other vegetation. Stems erect to 60cm. Leaves narrow, deeply furrowed on upperside towards base. Flowers inconspicuous, inflorescence elongating after flowering, June-Aug. Fruits 7-10mm, adpressed to axis of inflorescence.

Pondweed family *Potamogetonaceae*

Bog pondweed *Potamogeton polygonifolius*

Perennial found on the surface of peaty pools of water or very damp acidic ground. Floating leaves thick, broad and opaque with inconspicuous secondary veins, submerged leaves on longer stalks, blade narrowly elliptical; shape of leaves varying with depth of water, often tinged reddish. Leaves bright green when found growing in moss or other damp vegetation. Flowers *very small* with no petals, just 4 green sepals, May-Oct.

Trees and shrubs, climbers and scramblers

This section includes all the trees and shrubs found in Westerdale as well as the climbing and scrambling species. Please note that height for the trees, as for any species, will be their maximum i.e. the height to which a specimen might grow in favourable conditions. Westerdale's specimens are often much shorter due to the prevailing winds and intense cold during the winter months.

Pine family *Pinaceae*

European larch *Larix decidua*

A *deciduous* conifer, to 45m. Leaves needles to 30mm long, no more than 1mm wide, in dense clusters on short shoots, with pale green stripes on either side of mid-rib on underside. Female cones oval, bracts not recurved at tip. Introduced to the UK from the Carpathian mountains by John Tradescant in 1620, found in the wild since the end of the nineteenth century but also widely planted.

Noble fir *Abies procera*

Aka red fir and Christmas tree. Can grow to 50m. Bark silvery grey. Leaves greyish green, densely packed needles, grooved above with two whitish bands beneath. Cones purplish brown with drooping green scales, growing at the top of trees. Introduced to the UK from the western United States by David Douglas in 1831.

Scots pine *Pinus sylvestris*

Can grow to 40m. Bark scaly at first but turning characteristic reddish orange with age. Leaves are needles *growing in pairs*, often twisted. Cones slim and tapered when closed. Native but also widely planted throughout the UK.

Norway spruce *Picea abies*

Aka spruce fir. Forming a neat spire to 50m. Bark coppery grey, cracking on old trees. Needles 4-sided, glossy green, on peg-like bases, with distinctive smell. Cones cylindrical, 12-15cm, hanging downwards but not produced until the tree is about 40 years old. Popular as Christmas trees since Prince Albert introduced the custom in 1841.

Sitka spruce *Picea sitchensis*

Broadly conical tree to 60m. Bark purplish grey developing scaly plates. Foliage bluish grey, needles *flattened* with two white bands beneath and narrower lines above, straight and *very* spiny. Cones short, to 10cm. Indifferent to windy weather so a very hardy tree. Introduced to the UK in 1831, Westerdale's specimen was planted within a farmland 'snow hedge', to prevent drifting, in the early 1980s.[1]

Yew family *Taxaceae*

Yew *Taxus baccata*

Evergreen tree with multiple trunks thus appearing as a large shrub, to 20m. Bark reddish brown and flaking. Leaves linear, pointed, very dark green with two pale strips beneath, in two rows. Flowers greenish, Feb-April. Fruit a conspicuous fleshy red cup or aril. The churchyard yews would have been planted but they readily self-seed; some are probably several hundred years old. However, a yew can live for millennia, its wood said to outlive iron. It is believed that yew trees were of significance in pre-Christian times and their association with churchyards is because their sites were previously sacred, as was probably the case at Westerdale. Arils poisonous containing the toxins taxine and taxol.

---

1. With thanks to Colin Grice for this information.

Juniper family *Cupressaceae*

Common juniper *Juniperus communis*

In spite of its name this is far from common now due to changes in land management. Greyish bush to 8m. Bark greyish brown. Leaves to 1cm, in threes, tightly packed along branches. Flowers dioecious. Fruit a black berry taking three years to ripen. Native. In Westerdale berries have been collected for controlled germination and then children from Castleton School have helped to plant out young trees in an attempt to preserve local stock. Berries used in the making of gin and other spirits.

Bay family *Lauraceae*

Bay *Laurus nobilis*

Aka sweet bay, bay laurel and poet's laurel. Can grow to 20m but tends to be much bushier in colder conditions. Bark smooth. Leaves 5-12cm, smooth and shiny, stiff to the touch with wavy margins, aromatic. Flowers dioecious, bright yellow in spring. Fruit a black berry. Introduced to Britain from the Mediterranean in 1562. Used for culinary and medicinal purposes. Single specimen planted along one of the local lanes in the 1980s.[2] The bay tree was sacred to the Greek god Apollo whose temple at Delphi had its roof made entirely of bay leaves as protection against disease, witchcraft and lightning. A wreath of bay leaves came to symbolise excellence for poets and athletes. For the Romans, bay symbolised wisdom and glory. Laureate means 'crowned with laurels', hence poet laureate and baccalaureate.

Gooseberry family *Grossulariaceae*

Flowering currant *Ribes sanguineum*

Deciduous shrub to 2.5m. Leaves 3-10cm, hairy with 3-5 shallow lobes and deep veins giving a wrinkled appearance, usually scented when crushed. Flowers bright pink in drooping raceme, April-June. Fruit 6-10mm, purplish black berry with white bloom. Introduced to the UK from western United States in 1895. A garden escape.

Gooseberry *Ribes uva crispa*

Deciduous spiny shrub to 1m. Leaves 2-5cm, lobed and toothed, usually hairy, not scented. Flowers in tight groups of up to 3, greenish yellow, sometimes tinged with red, March-May. Fruit the familiar green or reddish gooseberry. Naturalised as a relic of cultivation.

2. With thanks to Colin Grice for this information.

Pea family *Fabaceae*

Gorse *Ulex europaeus*

Aka furze and whin. Densely spiny evergreen shrub to 2m. Spines rigid, deeply furrowed. Flowers bright yellow, sepals 2/3 length of corolla, with spreading hairs, mainly Feb-June. Fruit a dark pod that can be heard ejecting seeds on a warm day. Native. During mild winters gorse flowers throughout the year so it is said that when gorse is in bloom, kissing is in season!

Broom *Cytisis scoparius*

Much-branched *spineless* shrub to 2m. Stems with deep ridges. Leaves trifoliate, densely hairy with hairs appearing like a halo around leaf margins. Flowers deep yellow 15-20mm, May-June. Fruit a black, hairy pod ejecting seeds with a loud 'pop'. Native. Its tough but flexible branches were once used as brooms, hence its common name. Used for medicinal purposes by the Anglo-Saxons.

Laburnum *Laburnum anagyroides*

Aka golden rain. Tree to 8m. Young twigs and leaves densely downy, appearing silvered. Leaves trifoliate, leaflets oval. Flowers in pendulous racemes 15-30cm, May-June. Fruits ridged pods, **very poisonous**. Introduced, here a garden escape. Westerdale's specimen grows with its trunk fused with that of a rowan tree.

Rose family *Rosaceae*

Many-flowered rose *Rosa multiflora*

Aka multi-flowered rose and baby rose. Scrambler to 5m. Leaves with 5-9 leaflets and much divided, hairless stipules. Flowers 20-30mm, usually white in clusters of 10 or more, June-July. Hips small and bristly. Probably a garden escape, now naturalised in one hedgerow in the dale, recorded in Westerdale since 1950.

The following five species, as well as the hybrids, can be difficult to determine with certainty. They are best identified after the hips form when the differences are more apparent.[3]

3. With thanks to Vincent Jones for help with identifying these species.

Dog rose *Rosa canina*

Scrambling briar 3-4m with sturdy curved prickles. Leaves shiny, dark green, sometimes downy on underside. 5 sepals, 2 whiskered on both sides, 2 smooth, 1 whiskered on one side. Flowers fragrant to 6cm, pale pink, sometimes white, June-July. Hips on long stalks, bright red, oval, usually hairless, *losing sepals before ripening*. Dog roses have a long association with humans; rich in vitamin C, remains

of dog rose hips have been found at prehistoric dwelling sites; hips were collected during World War II for the production of rose hip syrup.

A short rhyme helps to remember the details of the five-sepalled calyx:

On a summer's day in sultry weather
Five brethren were born together
Two had beards and two had none
And the other had but half of one.

Occasionally a mossy growth can be seen at the top of a stem of *Rosa canina*. This is caused by the gall wasp *Diplolesis rosae*. The female wasp lays her eggs between the scales of the leaf bud, the plant gradually responds to this and eventually forms the mossy gall.[4] In view of their appearance much folklore has been attached to these fascinating forms. Traditionally they were believed to have been created by the woodland sprite Robin Goodfellow hence are often known as Robin's pincushions. Their common name, bedeguar gall, is from the French *bédegar* originally from the Persian *bād-āwar* meaning wind brought. Like many galls, their life cycle is complex.

Glaucous dog rose *Rosa vosagiaca*

Very similar to common dog rose but with reddish stems. Leaves smooth and *hairless*, folded in at mid-rib. Single bushes spreading and open rather than dense, June-July.

Hairy dog rose *Rosa corymbifera*

Stems arching to 2-3m, reddish green, with strong curved prickles. Leaves with wrinkled surface, hairy below. Flowers 3-5cm, June-July.

4. With thanks to Tom Higginbottom for this information.

Northern downy rose *Rosa mollis*

Aka soft downy rose. Upright suckering stems to 1.5m. Prickles straight and slender. Leaves greyish beneath with soft hairs. Flowers 3-4.5cm, deep pink rarely white, June-July. Hips on short stalks, *sepals upright and persistent.*

Sherard's rose *Rosa sherardii*

Aka Sherard's downy rose. Arching stems to 1.5m. Prickles slender with slight curve. Leaves bluish green. Flowers 2.5-4cm, usually deep pink, occasionally white, June-July. Hips with *spreading sepals,* persistent until ripe, falling before decay.

Rose hybrid *Rosa canina x Rosa caesia*

A common rose hybrid, even when one of the parent species absent, in this case *Rosa caesia.*

Rose hybrid *Rosa vosagiaca x Rosa sherardii*

Japanese rose *Rosa rugosa*

Erect, densely prickly, deciduous shrub to 1.5m. Leaves dark green, leaflets wrinkled above, downy beneath. Flowers 2-2.5cm, bright pink, June-July. Hips large, rounded, sepals persistent.

Bramble *Rubus* spp

Ubiquitous scrambler along hedgerows. Very prickly perennial. Leaves with toothed leaflets. Flowers 20-32mm, May-Nov. Sepals turn down in fruit. Fruit the well-known edible blackberry. A very familiar hedgerow plant but a critical genus with over 300 microspecies recognised, which are difficult to identify. Those found in Westerdale are listed here for interest.[5]

Rubus armeniacus R. ulmifolius
R. dasphyllus R. warenii
R. lindebergii

---

5. With thanks to Vincent Jones for this information.

Bird cherry *Prunus padus*

Aka hawkberry and hagberry. Tree to 15m. Bark dull grey tinged with purple. Leaves hairless, pointed and toothed with fine serrations. Petioles hairless, *red* with characteristic cherry glands. Flowers creamy white, fragrant, in pendant racemes 10-16cm, May-June. Fruit a bitter black cherry often eaten by birds before ripening. Usually found growing along water's edge.

Wild cherry *Prunus avium*

Aka gean and mazzard. Tree to 30m with smooth reddish bark peeling in strips. Petioles *green*. Leaves oval, pointed, slightly downy below, often coppery when young and turning rich colours in autumn with characteristic cherry glands at the base of the leaf. Flowers 15-25mm, petals very slightly notched, March-May. Fruit round, reddish, can be sweet or tart, often eaten by birds.

Some hard wood trees are attacked by a bracket fungus. The orange one, seen here on wild cherry, is *Laetiporus sulphureus* known as chicken-of-the-woods.[6] Its bright orange surface has a suede-like texture. It is a brown rot fungus which attacks the heartwood of the tree.

6. With thanks to David Barlow for this identification.

Blackthorn *Prunus spinosa*

Suckering bush often used as hedging but can grow to 4m. Whole plant with *very sharp* stiff thorns. Bark rough, purplish black. Leaves oval, matt green, finely toothed. Flowers 10-15mm appearing *before* leaves, March-May. Fruit a round purple plum with white bloom used for making sloe gin.

Blackthorn hybrid

P. spinosa x *P. domestica* = *Prunus* x *fruiticans*

Intermediate between parent species.

Damson *Prunus domestica* ssp *institia*

Small tree to 8m. Leaves with fine down on both sides. Flowers white sometimes green-tinged, April-May. Fruit rounded, purple 2-3cm. Used for making damson cheese.

Plum *Prunus domestica* ssp *domestica*

Aka bullace. Dense tree to 10m. *Very variable.* Twigs matt, downy when young. Leaves oval, finely toothed. Petiole with characteristic cherry glands. Flowers 15-25mm, off-white often tinged with green, April-May. Fruit an oval plum- purple, red or green. Possibly native but may have been introduced by the Romans.

Crab apple *Malus sylvestris*

Spiny tree to 10m. Leaves pointed, oval with fine teeth, downy when young. Flowers 30-40mm, pale pink, darker on under- side of petals, April-May. Fruit a small *very tart* apple, 20-30mm often remaining on tree until spring. Used for making crab apple jelly.

Hawthorn *Crataegus monogyna*

Aka quickset, quickthorn, white thorn and May. Usually used as a hedging plant but can grow to 15m, Westerdale trees *much* shorter. Leaves to 6cm, with 3-5 *deeply cut* lobes toothed at tips. Flowers 8-15mm, with prominent pink anthers and *one* style, petals occasionally tinged with pink, April-June. Fruit the familiar haws with *one stone*, collected for the school nature table if not eaten by the birds. Country children used to call this 'bread and cheese' and would nibble the leaves for a snack. 'Ne'er cast a clout till May be out' could refer to the plant as well as the month. Used for centuries for stock-proof hedging.

Wild raspberry *Rubus idaeus*

Upright perennial with biennial canes to 1.5m with occasional slender prickles. Leaves trifoliate, downy below. Flowers to 10mm with drab white petals that soon fall, growing in clusters, June-Aug. Fruit the familiar juicy berry with numerous segments. Native.

Rowan *Sorbus aucuparia*

Aka mountain ash. Tree to 18m. Leaves *alternate*, pinnate with narrow toothed leaflets, hairy below. Flowers 8-10mm, foetid, forming domed clusters, May-June. Fruits 6-9mm, orange-red berries tending to droop as they

ripen. Locally common, often seen near former settlements as believed to ward off evil. This tree was particularly sacred to the Druids.

Diels' cotoneaster *Cotoneaster dielsianus*

Arching, deciduous shrub to 3m. Leaves 1.5-2.5cm, veins slightly impressed on upper side, greyish beneath. Flowers several together, anthers white. Fruits round bright reddish orange berries. Garden escape. Aka Chinese cotoneaster as originally from Asia. The genus name *Cotoneaster* derives from *cotoneum*, Latin for quince; the suffix *-aster* means resembling.

Elm family *Ulmaceae*

Wych elm *Ulmus glabra*

Tree with rounded crown, rarely suckering. Bark smooth and grey turning greyish brown with age. Buds hairy, purplish black, flowers a tuft of reddish stamens well before the leaves, March-April. Leaves larger than any other native tree, to 18cm with 12-18 pairs of veins, midrib prominent below, upper surface coarse to the touch, base asymmetrical with longer lobe almost covering petiole. Fruit a single winged *centrally positioned* seed.

English elm *Ulmus procera*

Aka common elm. Tall tree to 38m with rough ridged bark. Leaves fairly scrubby above, puckered and crumpled, finely downy beneath, more rounded than wych elm. Fruit with off-centre, winged seed but flowers and fruit now rarely seen. Mature trees lost in the 1970s and 80s due to Dutch Elm Disease; a few small suckers still to be found.

Beech family *Fagaceae*

Beech *Fagus sylvatica*

Tree to 40m with broad trunk and smooth grey bark with *horizontal* markings. Young twigs downy and drooping becoming smooth and rigid with maturity. Leaves rounded ovals with crinkly margins, often retained throughout the winter. Flowers greenish tassels, male stalked and hanging, female unstalked and upright, May. Fruit a brown 3-sided nut, known as mast, held in a bristly husk. Beech mast was traditionally used for feeding pigs but the nuts have also been used for human food in famine years and beech nut oil can be extracted for cooking. Native but also widely planted. In ideal conditions can grow into magnificent specimens.

English oak *Quercus robur*

discolour or disfigure parts of the tree they do not cause lasting damage.

The spangle gall wasp (*Neuroterus quercusbaccarum*) creates disc-shaped galls on the underside of the leaves. An oak leaf can host up to 100 galls, each containing a single larva. The oak apple gall wasp (*Biorhiza pallida*) causes the development of globular galls, up to 5cm in diameter, housing as many as 30 gall wasp larvae. Other gall wasp larvae may parasitise the oak apple.

The knopper gall wasp (*Andricus quercuscalicis*), which became established in the UK during the 1970s, lays eggs in the developing acorns of pedunculate oak trees. The acorn and its cup then becomes distorted, converted into a ridged, woody structure in which the gall wasp larva develops. The next generation forms inconspicuous galls on the male catkins of the Turkey oak (*Quercus cerris*).

The marble gall wasp (*Andricus kollari*) causes hard spherical galls, up to 25mm in diameter, to form on twigs. They can persist for several years. They contain tannins, used in the production of leather; they are also used for ink. Many well-known documents including Magna Carta, the American Declaration of Independence as well as the Dead Sea Scrolls were all written with marble gall ink.

Aka pedunculate oak. Long-lived tree to 40m with sturdy trunk and broad crown. Bark greyish, developing rough ridges with age. Leaves deeply lobed, usually broader at base, basal lobes overlapping the *very short* petiole. Male flowers yellowish drooping catkins, female small and solitary, April-May. Fruit the familiar acorn in a scaly cup, usually in pairs on stalks 2-3cm, but only produced once the tree is 40-50 years old. A valuable timber tree used for ships and barrels as well as buildings.

English oaks can live to 1,000 years and achieve massive girth; most live 200-300 years. They host a wide variety of insects and other small creatures, supporting more wildlife than any other native species. Over 30 species of gall wasp are known to visit oak trees.[7] Although they may

7. With thanks to Tom Higginbottom for information on oak galls.

Oak hybrid *Quercus x rosacea*

A cross between English oak and sessile oak (*Quercus petraea*). Intermediate between the two species.

Turkey oak *Quercus cerris*

Long-lived tree to 40m. Similar to English oak but leaves more deeply divided and with *more-pointed lobes*. Bark grey with deep fissures. Buds have twisted whiskers. Fruit a *sessile* acorn in a *bristly* cup. Native of the Balkans and Syria, introduced to the UK in 1735, now naturalised.

Birch family *Betulaceae*

Alder *Alnus glutinosa*

Riverside tree to 20m but often shorter and bushy. Bark with vertical fissures. Buds often purplish, leaves 4-10cm, never pointed, usually with indented ends. Male catkins wine-red, female flowers short and stubby. Cones small, rounded, persisting for months. Wood formerly used for clog making and charcoal for gunpowder.

Leaves sometimes attacked by the alder leaf gall mite *Eriophyes laevis*, which produces lumps and bumps on the surface of the leaves, most often seen Aug-Sept.

Downy birch *Betula pubescens*

Short-lived tree to 25m. Bark greyish brown at first, later whitening. Twigs *downy, not weeping*. Leaves *evenly* toothed and rounder than silver birch, *downy* beneath, on *downy* stalks. Flowers in yellowish catkins, male longer and drooping, female firmer and erect, April-May. Fruit a single twin-winged nut, wings longer than style. The most common birch found on the moors.

Silver birch *Betula pendula*

Short-lived tree to 30m. Bark reddish at first but soon turning white then developing characteristic rough black markings, turning papery and peeling. Shoots *hairless*, leaves *hairless* on *hairless* stalks. Twigs soon *weeping*. Leaves triangular, *irregularly* toothed tapering to point at tip. Catkins and fruits similar to downy birch. During the Middle Ages birch tree wine was made from the spring sap, birch was also used in church decoration especially for midsummer day. A bracket fungus (*Fomitopsis betulinus*) can sometimes be seen on dead and damaged birch

trees.[8] Aka birch polypore and razor strop fungus as the velvety surface was traditionally used to smooth the edge of a razor. This bracket fungus was first described in 1788 and named *Boletus betulinus*, later it was renamed *Piptoporus betulinus* but in 2016 was given its current name in the light of modern molecular study. The fruiting body, seen here, can last for up to a year; it becomes corky with age. The fungal spores are held on the underside. The fungus itself can harbour a variety of insects. Birch polypore is an edible brown rot fungus i.e. once established it will cause the tree to rot. It has been used extensively in traditional medicine and the fungus was carried by Otzi the Iceman, the 5,300-year-old mummy found in Tyrol.

---

8. With thanks to David Barlow for this identification.

Hazel *Corylus avellana*

Tall shrub to 6m. Bark reddish brown, smooth and peeling. Leaves 5-12cm, rounded, often purplish when young. Flowers appearing before leaves. Male catkins visible in bud from Oct, becoming the familiar lambs' tails in early spring. Female flowers very small with bright pink styles looking like tassels, Jan-March. Fruit an edible nut encased in jagged, lobed husk. Formerly within a separate family *Corylaceae*.

Willow family *Salicaceae*

Aspen *Populus tremula*

Tree to 20m. Bark greyish brown, smooth. Twigs and buds downy when young. Leaves with wavy margins, paler beneath; flattened stalk causes leaf to tremble in the slightest breeze. Male and female catkins on same tree, male thicker, female longer. Suckers can create small colonies as here at Westerdale.

The following willows have been found in Westerdale. *Salix* species can be difficult to identify, best done when in leaf rather than in flower. They also readily hybridise.[9]

Bay willow *Salix pentandra*

Dense tree to 20m. Bark dark grey with criss-cross ridges. Shoots glossy green, hairless. Leaves *hairless*, smooth and shiny with very fine teeth - similar to bay, hence its common name. Catkins yellow on leafy shoots in spring, often opening with the leaves.

9. I am very grateful to Vincent Jones for help in identification of the willows.

Crack willow *Salix x fragilis*

Usually a stream- or river-side tree. Can grow to 25m but often pollarded. Bark with grey fissures; hairless twigs that snap easily making the familiar 'crack'. Broken off twigs will often root themselves in wet mud and soon grow. Leaves lanceolate, finely toothed with asymmetrical tip, bright green above, paler beneath. Catkins slender on short leafy stalks, April-May. Archaeophyte.

Goat willow *Salix caprea*

Aka common sallow. Tree or tall shrub to 10m. Twigs *smooth under the bark*. Leaves short and broad, 5-12cm long and 3-8cm across, soft to the touch but losing hairs with age. Catkins short, more or less unstalked, with dark scales, March-May, before the leaves.

Grey willow *Salix cinerea* ssp *oleifolia*

Aka grey sallow and pussy willow. Small tree to 10m often more shrub like. Young twigs hairy with *ridges under the bark*. Leaves obovate, persistently hairy below. Catkins short, more or less stalkless, March-April. Native, common throughout the North York Moors.

Willow hybrid *Salix cinerea x caprea = S. x reichardtii*

This hybrid between goat and grey willow is common.

Willow hybrid *Salix cinerea x aurita = S. x multinervis*

Willow hybrid *Salix cinerea x viminalis = S. x holosericea*

Osier *Salix viminalis*

Tall shrub or small tree to 6m. Young twigs hairy, becoming glabrous. Leaves long and *very narrow*, dark green, glabrous above but covered in white silky hairs below, margins untoothed and in-rolled beneath. Catkins bright yellow, appearing before leaves, March-April, male short, more or less stalkless, female longer. Grown for its long flexible twigs (withies) used for basket making. Archaeophyte. It is possible that the name Osseker Crook in Westerdale derives from the place where osiers were grown for baskets and hurdles.

Willows were traditionally used for church decoration for Palm Sunday, the catkin-bearing willow being regarded as the English palm.

Maple family *Sapindaceae*

Horse-chestnut *Aesculus hippocastanum*

Familiar ornamental tree to 40m. Leaves palmate with 5-7 leaflets. In early spring *sticky* buds develop, beloved of school nature tables. Flowers white, occasionally pink, with a yellow spot, 4-5 petals in unmistakable 'candles' to 30cm, May-June. Fruit a shiny brown nut held inside a fleshy, spiny case, used by country children in 'conker' fights. Introduced around 1616, native to Macedonia and Albania, now naturalised in the English countryside. The natural chemical *aescin* is extracted from the tree and is used to treat aches and pains, bruises and strains in both horses and humans.

Sycamore *Acer pseudoplatanus*

Deciduous spreading tree to 30m. Bark pinkish grey, smooth at first becoming fissured with age. Leaves 10-15cm, few hairs in vein axils below, lobes with irregular teeth. Flowers 5-6mm across with 5 sepals and 5 petals in pendulous inflorescence, May-June. Fruit the familiar winged seed, playthings of country children who flick them as 'helicopters'. Introduced, possibly by the Romans or maybe later in Tudor times, but now completely naturalised.

Nasturtium family *Tropaeolaceae*

Flame flower *Tropaeolum speciosum*

Aka flame nasturtium. Hardy, herbaceous perennial with wiry stems to 3m. Scrambles over plants to find sunlight, flowers prolifically. Leaves palmately lobed with 5-7 obovate leaflets. Funnel-shaped, spurred flowers grow on long stalks arising from leaf axils. After flowering the red calyces turn back to reveal three blue berries. From Chile, *Tropaeolum speciosum* is often difficult to establish but here it has become naturalised along the churchyard yew hedge. When dormant over the winter, a flame flower plant retreats to an underground tuber where it is largely protected from frost, which is how Westerdale's splendid specimen has been able to survive. It is not known how this came to be here but has been well established for several decades.

Ash family *Oleaceae*

Ash *Fraxinus excelsior*

Deciduous tree to 25m. Bark grey, smooth at first becoming fissured with age. Buds sooty black appearing before the year's end. Leaves pinnate with 7-13 toothed leaflets. Flowers, without petals, appear before leaves, in dense axillary clusters, March-May. Fruits the familiar ash 'keys'. Ash timber is used for baseball bats, bows and for tool handles so is of considerable economic importance. Sadly some UK trees are now affected by ash die-back caused by the fungus *Hymenoscyphus fraxineus*.

Lilac *Syringa vulgaris*

Erect suckering shrub to 7m. Leaves simple, margins entire. Flowers sweetly scented, white, mauve or deep purple, in large terminal, pyramidal panicles. Individual flowers 1.5-2cm, with 4 petals united into a 4-lobed tube. Introduced, often grown in gardens from where they spread by suckering, as here.

Holly family *Aquifoliaceae*

Holly *Ilex aquifolium*

Familiar dioecious evergreen to 15m. Bark grey and smooth sometimes with small warts. Leaves thick and glossy with wavy margins usually with sharp spines, older taller trees tend to have leaves without spines. Flowers with 4 sepals and 4 white petals, female with single central style, May-Aug. The familiar red berries develop following the female flowers. From prehistoric times to the eighteenth century holly was an important winter animal fodder; holly leaves have a high calorific value as well as being rich in nutrients. The name Hollins in Westerdale probably signifies the site of a holly wood used for winter feed especially for sheep. In the nineteenth century holly was used for driving whips as well as for bobbins for the cotton mills.

Honeysuckle family *Caprifoliaceae*

Honeysuckle *Lonicera periclymenum*

Aka woodbine. Deciduous woody climber to 7m, twining clockwise. Leaves oval, green above, greyish beneath, appearing very early in the year. Flowers 40-50mm, very fragrant, often tinged with pink; two lips forming a tube with protruding stamens, June-Sept. Fruit a poisonous red berry. Used in pot pourri and at one time used for medicinal purposes.

Elder *Sambucus nigra*

Deciduous bush to 10m. Bark greyish with corky cross ridges. Leaves dark green, in opposite pairs with 5 or 7 toothed leaflets. Creamy aromatic flowers in flat-topped clusters, May-Aug. Fruits edible black berries on red stalks. Both flowers and berries still used for culinary purposes. Once called 'the medicine chest of the country people' as it had so many other uses as well as being part of ancient folklore.

A jelly-like fungus can sometimes be seen on the branches of elder. *Auricularia auricula-judae* is known as Jew's ear, wood ear or jelly ear. Its fruiting body, seen here darkening with age, does appear jelly-like. It grows on both dead and living specimens of several deciduous species but prefers elder. It acquired its common name because it was believed that Judas hanged himself from an elder tree and the fungus is to remind us of his death. In the West, jelly ear has been used in folk medicine for centuries and it is still eaten in China as well as being used in Chinese medicine. It has been shown to have anti-tumour, hypoglycemic, anti-coagulant and cholesterol-lowering properties.

Guelder-rose *Viburnum opulus*

Deciduous shrub to 4m. Leaves palmately lobed with irregular teeth, reddening in autumn. Flowers in flat-topped umbel-like clusters, outer flowers sterile with 5 showy petals, much larger than inner, fertile ones, May-July. Fruit a translucent red berry loved by the birds.

Viburnum *Viburnum x bodnantense*

Deciduous tree to 3m. Leaves oval, bronzed when young, maturing to dark green. Flowers fragrant, pink, in tight clusters, Dec-Feb. Garden escape.

Rushes, sedges and grasses

Rushes and sedges can be differentiated by remembering that *rushes are round and sedges have edges*. Sedges are usually triangular in cross section with leaves often keeled so are somewhat sharp to the touch.

Rush family *Juncaceae*

Soft rush *Juncus effusus*

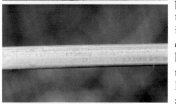

Densely tufted, stiffly upright perennial to 1.5m. Stems bright green, smooth and glossy with *continuous* pith and many inconspicuous longitudinal ridges. Inflorescence appears to grow from side of stem, spreading or compact. Tepals narrow with sharp points, June-Aug. Very common on moorland, especially in wet flushes, often forming large patches. Locally these were known as sieves (pronounced civvies). In ancient times rushes were used to create sieves. They were also once used for strewing on earth floors. Formerly peeled, except for one narrow strip of the green, and the inner pith soaked in fat and used for rush lights. A long, well-made rush light would burn for almost an hour.

Hard rush *Juncus inflexus*

Densely tufted glaucous perennial to 1.2m. Stiffly upright, dull, hairless, stems prominently ridged. Internal pith *interrupted*. Internal septa can be felt by running finger and thumb along leaves. Inflorescence appears to grow from side of stem, spreading. Tepals narrow, unequal, June-Aug. Does not like strongly acidic ground, usually found in calcareous grassland.

Compact rush *Juncus conglomeratus*

Densely tufted, erect perennial to 1m. Stems greyish green, matt rather than glossy, slightly bent above inflorescence. Inflorescence a tight head with many fine ridges on stem immediately below, May-July. Prefers acid ground.

Bulbous rush *Juncus bulbosus*

Aka lesser jointed rush. Very variable, slender perennial. Stems usually swollen at base, tufted, procumbent, often rooting at nodes. Leaves thread-like. Inflorescence spreading, sparse. Flowers with outer tepals acute, inner blunt, June-Sept. Usually on muddy ground, especially on edges of ditches.

Heath rush *Juncus squarrosus*

Densely tufted, wiry perennial to 50cm. Leaves *all basal*, stiff with deep channel along upper surface. Flowers in tight clusters on upright branches, lowest bract much shorter than inflorescence. Tepals dark brown, June-July. Common on moorland.

Jointed rush *Juncus articulatus*

Prostrate to upright perennial to 80cm. Leaves curved, compressed, with inconspicuous septa or joints (can be felt by running finger and thumb along leaf). Branches of terminal inflorescence spreading at acute angles, tepals very dark brown, June-Sept. Frequent in damp places, especially on track sides and in bare patches, less common on moorland.

Sharp-flowered rush *Juncus acutiflorus*

Stiffly upright perennial to 1m. Leaves ascending with conspicuous transverse septa. Inflorescence repeatedly branching at acute angles. Tepals tapering to fine point, July-Sept. Found on moorland, often forming large patches.

Toad rush *Juncus bufonius*

Upright or procumbent *annual* to 35cm. Stems sometimes much branched. Leaves dark green, bristle-like. Inflorescence leafy, repeatedly branched. Tepals green, pointed, June-Aug. Common in many habitats preferring bare places without competition.

Great wood-rush *Luzula sylvatica*

Easily identified, tall, robust perennial to 80cm. Leaves bright green, glossy, sparsely hairy especially along margins. Terminal inflorescence spreading, flowers brown, in groups of 3-5, tepals as long as capsule, May-June. Prefers stream edges, especially in woodland.

Hairy wood-rush *Luzula pilosa*

Upright, tufted, grass-like perennial to 30cm. Leaves sparsely hairy with characteristic slight swelling at tip. Flowers dark brown, single, on slender, spreading branches, April-June. Prefers bank sides in woodland but also occurs on moorland.

Heath wood-rush *Luzula multiflora*

Erect, densely tufted perennial to 40cm. Leaves grass-like, sparsely hairy. Flowers in sessile clusters or with short stalks, anthers as long as filaments, April-June. Found on acidic, marshy ground, usually on moorland.

Field wood-rush *Luzula campestris*

Aka Good Friday grass and sweeps' brooms. Low growing, upright, loosely tufted perennial to 15cm. Leaves narrow, grass-like with long white hairs. Inflorescence consists of 1 sessile and 3-6 stalked clusters of 3-12 flowers, tepals dark brown, anthers bright yellow, 3-4x as long as filaments, March-June. Prefers acid grassland.

Sedge family *Cyperaceae*

Common cottongrass *Eriophorum angustifolium*

Botanically speaking, this is not a grass but a member of the sedge family aka cotton sedge and bog cotton. Rhizomatous perennial to 75cm. Stems bluntly triangular in cross section. Leaves deeply channelled, narrowing to triangular tip with characteristic rust colour. Flowers in nodding head with pure white bristles, May-June. Found on moorland, creating cloud-like carpets.

Hare's tail cottongrass *Eriophorum vaginatum*

Tussock-forming perennial with smooth, bluntly triangular stems to 50cm. Similar to common cottongrass but much less frequent, flowers *solitary*, May-June.

Note: *Carex* species are more easily identified in fruit than in flower.

Common sedge *Carex nigra*

Aka black sedge. Tufted perennial to 70cm, stems rough, triangular in cross section. Leaves narrow, flat, tapering to fine point. Inflorescence with leaf-like bracts, male spike narrow above 1-4 female spikes with black glumes with green mid-ribs. Fruits green, becoming black. Found on damp grassland.

Glaucous sedge *Carex flacca*

Creeping, tufted perennial to 60cm. Leaves

distinctly *glaucous beneath*, tapering to fine channelled point. Bracts leaf-like, lowest almost as long as inflorescence. Flowers in characteristic spikes, 2-3 male spikes, 1-5 female spikes, topmost erect and sessile, *lower nodding*, May-June. Fruits green turning black, fruiting June-July. Common in a variety of habitats.

Carnation sedge *Carex panicea*

Creeping, tufted perennial to 60cm. Leaves distinctly *glaucous on both sides*, tapering to solid, 3-angled tip. Inflorescence with 1 male spike, and 1-3 reddish brown female spikes with green mid-ribs, May-June, Fruits smooth, swollen, olive green, June-July. Prefers wet flushes and bogs.

Oval sedge *Carex leporina*

Formerly *Carex ovalis*. Densely tufted perennial to 90cm, stems often curving. Inflorescence with yellowish-brown, tightly packed oval spikes, often overlapping, June. Fruits light brown, July-Aug. Usually found in grassland.

Pill sedge *Carex pilulifera*

Densely tufted perennial to 30cm. Stems wiry and arching, leaves narrow, tapering. Inflorescence clustered, lowest bract leaf-like. Spikes sessile, 1 male spike, 2-4 female spikes, ovoid, May-June. Fruits green, ovoid, hairy at tip, June-July. Common on moorland.

Remote sedge *Carex remota*

Densely tufted, slender perennial to 60cm. Stems *arching*, bluntly three-angled. Leaves narrow, pale green. Flowers in June, 4-7 spikes, male and female together, well separated i.e. remote, hence it common name. Lowest bract longer than inflorescence. Fruits green, July-Aug. Found in wet places especially by woodland stream edges.

© Nan Sykes

Star sedge *Carex echinata*

Densely tufted perennial to 40cm. Stems bluntly three-angled, spreading. Flowers in knots of 2-5 spikes separated along stem, May-June. Fruits yellowish brown, spreading to give characteristic *star-like* appearance, July-Aug.

Flea sedge *Carex pulicaris*

Distinctive sedge, short stems rounded to 30cm. Leaves dark green, very narrow, keeled with blunt tips. Male flower upright in terminal spike, female spreading. Fruits dark brown and shiny, *down-turned* when ripe, springing off the stem when touched, like fleas, hence the common name. Found in wet flushes.

Common yellow sedge *Carex demissa*

Stems to 30cm, somewhat rounded, usually with curving habit, tensely tufted. Leaves usually nearly as long as stems, rigid and sharply keeled. Bracts tend to stick out at right angles. Male spike narrow at top of stem, female in clusters, one lower than the rest on a longer stalk. Fruits 3-4mm, greenish and faintly ribbed, June-Sept. Found in wet flushes and acidic bogs.

Greater tussock-sedge *Carex paniculata*

Extremely robust densely tufted perennial forming large tussocks up to 1.5m tall and 1m across. Leaves sturdy with sharply toothed margins. Inflorescence up to 15cm, dusty brown, May-June. Fruits green to dark brown, July-Aug. Found in rough pasture and woodland. The specimens in Westerdale are likely to be several decades old.

Lesser pond sedge *Carex acutiformis*

Sturdy, tufted plant with far-creeping rhizomes. Whole plant with a rough feel to it. Stems 60-150cm, sharply three-angled, slightly flanged. Leaves to 160cm, keeled or even pleated, drooping at tips. Ligule long and acute. Inflorescence 2-3 male spikes above with 3-4 female below, with bract extending beyond inflorescence. Fruits ellipsoid, ribbed with short notched beak, July-Sept. Found by pond edges and in wet meadowland.

Bristle club-rush *Isolepis setacea*

Tufted annual to 15cm, often much shorter. Leaves bristle-like, shorter than flowering stems. Flowers made up of sessile spikelets, bracts stem-like and much longer than inflorescence, May-July. Fruit a shiny nut with longitudinal ridges. Found scattered along sides of ditches.

Common spike-rush *Eleocharis palustris*

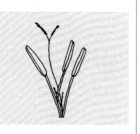

Easily overlooked perennial with far-creeping rhizomes that bear cylindrical stems 10-60cm, sometimes singly, sometimes in small tufts, each with an oval spikelet. Leaves reduced to tubular sheaths around stem. Spikelets with short bristles, May-July. Fruit a nut 1-2mm long, style base swollen, four bristles usually remaining. Found in marshes, wet grassland and shallow fresh water.

Grass family *Poaceae* (formerly *Graminaea*)

Creeping bent *Agrostis stolonifera*

Creeping grass, rooting at nodes. Upright stems to 40cm. Leaves flat with *blunt* ligules. Spikelets usually without awns, panicle contracting in fruit, June-Aug. Very common, varying habitats.

Common bent *Agrostis capillaris*

Formerly *Agrostis tenuis*. Tufted grass, 20-50 cm. Leaves tapering to fine point, flat and rough with *short blunt* ligules. Spikelets without awns, June-Aug. Common in short grassland.

Velvet bent *Agrostis canina*

Tufted grass, 20-60cm with leafy runners rooting at nodes. Leaves narrow, rough with *pointed* ligules. Spikelets usually with long awns, June-Aug. Scattered in wet bare ground.

Soft brome *Bromus hordaceus* ssp *hordaceus*

Variable, soft, hairy annual to 80cm (often much shorter). Leaves flat. Panicle greyish green, erect with tapering, often hairy spikelets tightly packed together, drooping to one side at maturity, June-Aug.

Barren brome *Anisantha sterilis*

Formerly *Bromus sterilis*. Pendulous annual to 1m. Leaves flat, downy with hairy sheaths, ligules toothed, 2-4mm. Stems smooth, hairless. Panicle loose and drooping with rough branches each with only one awned spikelet. Spikelets purplish when ripe, May-June.

Great brome *Anisantha diandra*

Loosely tufted annual to 80cm. Inflorescence spreading and nodding, branches in clusters of 2-4. Spikelets 7-9cm including long awns, May-July.

Rye brome *Bromus secalinus*

Loosely tufted annual to 80cm. Similar to soft brome, *qv*, but with spikelets more spreading, June-July. An arable weed, rare in Westerdale.

Cock's-foot *Dactylis glomerata*

Sturdy perennial in dense tufts to 1m, common along roadsides. Leaves rough, up to 1cm wide, ligules jagged 2-10mm long. Panicle comprises clusters of bristly, awned spikelets on stiff branches the lowest of which spreads at c 45° to main stem giving characteristic cock's foot appearance, May-Sept.

Crested dog's tail *Cynosurus cristatus*

Wiry, tufted perennial to 60cm, usually much shorter. Leaves smooth and flat with tight, straw-coloured leaf sheath. Panicle dense, characterised by spikelets on one side only, June-Aug.

Meadow fescue *Schedonorus pratensis*

Formerly *Festuca pratensis*. Slender grass to 80cm, usually shorter. Leaves narrow, 4mm, leaf sheath smooth, auricles and ligules small, June-July. Occasionally hybridises with perennial rye grass (*Lolium perenne*).

Red fescue *Festuca rubra* ssp *rubra*

Very variable, tufted perennial to 80cm. Basal leaves very fine with leaf sheath *completely closed* at first. Spikelets with awns, May-July.

Sheep's fescue *Festuca ovina*

Tufted perennial to 40cm, often much shorter. Leaves narrow, bristle-like and rough, ligules very short. Awns very short, May-June.

Fine-leaved sheep's fescue *Festuca filiformis*

Similar to sheep's fescue but with leaf sheaths split to base. Spikelets usually without awns.

Marsh foxtail *Alopercurus geniculatus*

Creeping, occasionally floating perennial. Stems have 'knees' at lower nodes, which sometimes set roots. Leaves smooth, flat with spreading blades, leaf sheath inflated. Panicle dense, spikelets blunt with short awns, June-Aug. Usually found in mud or shallow pools.

Meadow foxtail *Alopecurus pratensis*

Tufted perennial to 1m. Stems smooth, leaves flat with smooth sheaths. Panicle cylindrical, gingerish and soft, looking like a small fox's brush. Spikelets pointed, slightly hairy with short awns, April-June. Very common.

Couch grass *Elytrigia repens*

Formerly *Elymus repens*, aka twitch; a gardener's nightmare. Sturdy, erect perennial to 120cm, spreading by far-reaching rhizomes difficult to eradicate. Leaves flat with hairs above, sheaths round and smooth with pointed auricles, ligules short. Panicle slender with overlapping spikelets in two opposite rows on stem, spreading at right angles *not* in same plane (*cf* rye-grasses). Spikelets sometimes with awns, June-Aug. Very common.

Annual meadow grass *Poa annua*

Low growing annual, tending to sprawl, to 30cm. Leaves bright green with blunt ligules and flattened sheaths. Panicle spreading, lower branches often down-turned. Spikelets pale green occasionally pinkish, crowding around outer half of branches, Jan-Dec. One of the world's most successful plants, found on every continent. It is adaptable and aggressive and can out-compete many other species. It is listed as a cosmopolitan weed in the *Global Compendium of Weeds*.

Smooth meadow grass *Poa pratensis*

Tufted grass to 40cm. Stems *smooth*, ligules *blunt to 5mm*. Panicle much branched, May-July. In the USA this is known as Kentucky blue grass.

Rough meadow grass *Poa trivialis*

Single-stemmed perennial to 60cm. Stems *rough* (run fingers *down* stem), ligules *pointed to 10mm*. Panicle branches in spreading whorls, each branch with 4-6 spikelets, June-July.

Spreading meadow grass *Poa humilis*

Perennial to 30cm, with extensive rhizomes; often overlooked as very similar to smooth meadow grass. *Produces scattered shoots and solitary flowering stems.* Leaves bluish grey, ligules short, rounded. Panicle *heavy-looking*, spreading, spikelets finely pointed, June-July.

Early hair-grass *Aira praecox*

Slender annual to 50cm. Leaves bristle-like with smooth sheaths, ligules blunt. Panicle dense, spike-like. An early flowerer and soon dries out to a golden colour, April-June.

Tufted hair-grass *Deschampsia cespitosa*

Tensely tufted, tussock-forming perennial to 2m. Leaves dark green, deeply ribbed on upper side, edges rough. Panicle bright green tending to bow to one side, awned spikelets, June-Aug.

Wavy hair-grass *Deschampsia flexuosa*

Tufted perennial to 70cm. Leaves bright green and bristle-like. Panicle with wavy branches, spikelets purplish brown, June-July. Found on moorland.

111

Mat-grass *Nardus stricta*

Wiry, tufted perennial, shoots densely packed at base, to 40cm. Leaves stiff, bristle-like, tightly rolled. Spikelets along one side of stem, greenish purple, June-Aug. Common on moorland.

Barley *Hordeum distichon*

Familiar, erect annual to 90cm. Leaves 1.5cm wide with pointed auricles, ligules very short. Inflorescence 6-12cm, spikelets with *very long* awns, May-June. A relic of cultivation.

Bread wheat *Triticum aestivum*

Annual to 1.5m. Leaves broad, sheath smooth with auricles, ligules blunt. Spikelets sturdy, plump, May-July. A relic of cultivation, no longer grown in Westerdale.

Cultivated oat *Avena sativa*

Tall, erect annual to 1.5m. Leaves broad, flat, tapering to fine point. Spikelets pendulous, usually without awns, July-Sept. A relic of cultivation. Once grown widely here; one of the early fourteenth century Templar documents relating to Westerdale records seed for 60 acres of oats.

False oat-grass *Arrhenatherum elatius*

Upright perennial to 1.8m. Leaves long, flat and pointed, sometimes hairy above. Panicle purplish green, shiny. Spikelets with one long bent awn, June-Sept.

Yellow oat-grass *Trisetum flavescens*

Loosely tufted, upright perennial to 80cm. Leaves long, flat and with finely pointed tip. Panicle shiny with characteristic yellowish tinge, branches clustered. Spikelets shiny, tips with 2 tiny teeth and 2 or 3 yellowish awns, May-July.

Perennial rye-grass *Lolium perenne*

Loosely tufted perennial with several tillers, to 90cm. Leaves *folded* at first, glossy green beneath with prominent mid-rib, base of sheath-reddish. Spikelets sessile, *in two rows in same plane* (cf couch grass), *without* awns, May-Aug. A valuable pasture grass, common along roadsides.

Italian rye-grass *Lolium multiflorum*

Annual or biennial, similar to perennial rye grass but without tillers at flowering, to 90cm. Leaves *rolled* (not folded) at first. Spikelets *with* awns, June-Aug. An occasional roadside grass.

Timothy *Phleum pratense*

Familiar, sturdy, upright perennial to 1.5m, stem usually swollen at nodes. Leaves rough, ligules long and blunt. Spikelets in tight 'microphone' head, short awns, June-Aug. Common along roadsides.

Sweet vernal grass *Anthoxanthum odoratum*

Short-lived perennial to 50cm smelling of new mown hay, hence its common name. Leaves flat, pointed with few fine hairs, sheaths with conspicuous ring of hairs at junction with leaf blade, ligules blunt. Spikelets with short awns (some bent, some straight), in dense spike-like panicle, April-June. Prefers mildly acidic grassland.

Small sweet-grass *Glyceria declinata*

Aka glaucous sweet-grass. Tufted perennial to 45cm. Leaves bluish green, sometimes tinged purple, short with hooded tip. Inflorescence slightly curved, branches *not spreading*. June-Sept. Usually found by muddy margins of ponds and ditches, especially where trampled by cattle, some leaves lying along surface of water.

Plicate sweet-grass *Glyceria notata*

Mat-forming perennial with prostrate or ascending stems to 75cm. Leaves long with hooded tip, sheaths keeled. Inflorescence *spreading*, much branched, *one branch longer than others*. Spikelets with blunt tips, June-Aug. Found in muddy pools.

Yorkshire fog *Holcus lanatus*

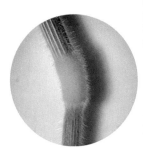

Softly hairy perennial to 1m. Stems and nodes downy. Leaves flat, greyish green, downy, ligules blunt. Leaf nodes somewhat swollen, sheaths usually with purple stripes. Panicle tinged pink giving a fog-like appearance when growing *en masse*, hence its common name. Spikelets with *slightly arching* awns, May-Sept.

Creeping soft-grass *Holcus mollis*

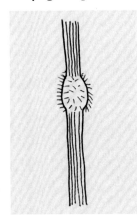

Similar to Yorkshire fog but with mat-forming creeping rhizomes. Stems more or less *hairless* but with 'bearded' nodes (hairy knees!). Spikelets with *straight* awns, June-Aug. Prefers well-drained acidic soil.

Quaking grass *Briza media*

Aka dothery docks.[1] An attractive, easily recognised perennial to 75cm, often much shorter. Leaves smooth, ligule rounded. Spikelets somewhat squat on hair-like branches which quiver in the wind, hence its common name, June-Aug. Prefers calcareous grassland.

Reed canary-grass *Phalaris arundinacea*

Tall, reed-like perennial to 2m usually found along river sides. Leaves broad, flat and tapering, ligules long often becoming torn. Spikelets densely clustered together in spike-like panicle, June-Aug. Beloved of harvest mice; the sturdy stems make ideal nesting sites.

---

1. With thanks to Anne Addison and the late Emma Beeforth for this information.

Reflexed saltmarsh-grass *Puccinellia distans*

Turf-forming perennial, usually with upright stems, to 60cm. Panicle branches becoming *reflexed on maturity*, spikelets towards end of branches, June-Aug. Frequent on verges due to road salt, found especially near grit mounds.

Heath-grass *Danthonia decumbens*

Flowering stems usually prostrate, 40-60cm. Distinguished by ring of hairs at top of leaf sheath and characteristic ligule, also a ring of hairs. Inflorescence a small panicle, spikelets with 4-6 flowers. Found on heaths and acidic grassland.

Ferns and horsetails

The following section includes the ferns and horsetails found in Westerdale.

Ferns and horsetails are non-flowering plants; they reproduce by spores and first appeared on earth many millions of years ago. In the horsetails the spores are held in terminal cones. In ferns the spores are held in sori on the underside of the leaves, known as fronds. The sori are often covered by a membrane known as the indusium. Fern fronds open gradually, curled in a characteristic fiddle-head formation at first.

Adder's tongue family *Ophioglossaceae*

Adder's tongue *Ophioglossum vulgatum*

Unmistakable, deciduous fern with a single sterile blade 4-15cm with erect petiole; fertile spike 1.5-5cm carrying 10-40 sporangia, ripe May-Aug. An indicator of old meadow land.

Horsetail family *Equisetaceae*

Field horsetail *Equisetum arvense*

Perennial to 80cm. Sterile stems green with 6-9 ridges, sheaths green with *spreading* green teeth, April-Oct. Fertile stems usually whitish, unbranched, April-May. Spores held in cones at top of fertile stems. Found along roadsides, can be a tiresome garden weed.

Wood horsetail *Equisetum sylvaticum*

Looking like a pale green Christmas tree to 50cm. Sterile stems with many drooping branches, sheaths loose, green with gingerish teeth, April-Nov. Fertile stems paler, unbranched at first, May. Found in damp woodland.

Water horsetail *Equisetum fluviatile*

Stems largely unbranched, to 1.5m. Sterile stems with yellowish green sheaths and whitish teeth; fertile stems with tight green sheaths and short black teeth, May-Nov. Cones blunt, spores ripen in June. Found growing in water.

Marsh horsetail *Equisetum palustre*

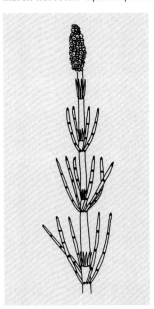

Slender stems 10-60cm with few prominent vertical ridges. Branches in irregular whorls, sheaths on main stem with erect black teeth. Sheaths on branches blunt, green with minute black tips. Cones terminal on main stem. More delicate looking than other horsetails. Found in wet flushes.

Bracken family

Dennstaedtiaceae (formerly *Hypolepidaceae*)

Bracken *Pteridium aquilinum*

Vigorous, long-lived deciduous fern. Fronds grow singly often over 2m long, 2-3x pinnate usually leathery and very tough. Spores ripe July-Sept. Often the dominant vegetation on moorland. Formerly important for animal bedding; many of the houses in Westerdale have rights of bracken, that is the right to cut bracken from common land, although few exercise that right these days.

Spleenwort family *Aspleniaceae*

Hart's tongue *Asplenium scolopendrium*

Unmistakable in its evergreen, undivided, strap-shaped fronds up to 60cm. Sori linear, 1-3cm, borne in pairs although appearing as singles, indusia opening towards centre of pair. Spores ripe July-Aug.

© David Barlow

Marsh fern family *Thelypteridaceae*

Lemon-scented fern *Oreopteris limbosperma*

Aka mountain fern. Deciduous bright green fronds 30-100cm borne in erect crown on stout ascending rhizomes. Fronds 1x pinnate with pinnae gradually reducing in length along rachis, shorter at base and apex. Segments untoothed, sori in two rows along margins. Spores ripe July-Aug. Citrus scent when crushed. Not to be confused with male fern (*Dryopteris filix-mas*) qv.

Lady fern family

Woodsiaceae (formerly *Arythriaceae*)

Lady fern *Athyrium filix-femina*

Pale green, arching fronds 20-100cm, 2x or 3x pinnate giving a feathery, delicate appearance. Sori in two rows down either side of mid-rib of pinnule, indusia crescent-shaped. Spores ripe July-Aug.

Hard fern family *Blechnaceae*

Hard fern *Blechnum spicant*

Unmistakable, sterile fronds 10-40cm form a rosette; fertile fronds 15-75cm upright looking like a fish backbone. Sori linear, one on each side of mid-rib of pinna. Spores ripe June-Aug.

Buckler fern family *Dryopteridaceae*

Broad buckler fern *Dryopteris dilitata*

© David Barlow

Triangular, dark green fronds 30-150cm borne in dense crown and arching downwards. Base of rachis covered in pointed scales with dark centres and pale margins. Spores ripe July-Sept.

Scaly male fern *Dryopteris affinis*

Fronds shiny, 50-150cm, somewhat leathery, often overwintering. *Black spot* where pinnae join rachis which is densely covered in orange scales. Pinnules more or less parallel sided, toothed only at blunt tip. Sori in sets of 4-5 along mid-rib of pinnule. Indusia convex, curved around sori, ripe July-Oct.

Male fern *Dryopteris filix-mas*

Fronds 40-90cm in large clumps with thick rhizomes. Sparse scales along rachis; 15-30 pinnae along rachis, *no* black spot where they join. Sori circular, up to 6 on each segment, ripe July-Aug. Roots of male fern used to be dug up on St John's Eve, 23rd June, and used to make a charm said to ward off evil spirits.

Liverwort family *Marchantiaceae*

Umbrella liverwort *Marchantia polymorpha*

Aka common liverwort. Not a flowering plant, fern or horsetail but a thallose liverwort, included here for interest. The leaf-like thalli grow to 10cm x 2cm, usually green but brown or purplish in older specimens. Plants produce umbrella-like gametophores – male and female on separate plants – which reproduce asexually. Thalli are often found on the tops of the earth in plant pots; thalli and gametophores can be found along the churchyard path at Westerdale.

Lichens

The following five images are of some of the lichens I have found in the process of writing this book. Lichens are composite organisms developing from a stable symbiotic relationship between a fungus and algae or cyanobacteria. There is still much debate about the nature of this symbiosis but the resulting organisms are different from their component parts. Throughout the world there are about 20,000 species of lichen. While some are plant-like, lichens are not plants but are included here for interest.[1]

Evernia prunastri

Parmelia sulcata

Hypogymnia physodes

The yellow one is *Xanthoria parietina* growing with *Hypogymnia physodes*.

This is a mix of *Cladonia* species including *C. chlorophaea*.

1. With many thanks to Joyce Scott for identifying the lichens.

Glossary

Achene: small dry, single-seeded fruit such as in buttercups and dandelions.

Actinomorphic: having more than one line of symmetry *cf* zygomorphic.

Adpressed: flattened against a stem or leaf.

Annual: a plant that germinates, flowers, sets seed and dies in one year *cf* biennial and perennial.

Anther: male part of a flower, producing the pollen.

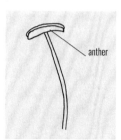

anther

Archaeophyte: a plant usually associated with human activity that may not be native but is long established, at least before 1500.

Aril: fleshy covering around a seed as in yew (*Taxus baccata*).

Auricle: ear-like growth at base of leaf, often clasping stem; see e.g. sow-thistle species.

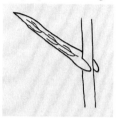

Awn: in grasses, stiff bristle growing from back of a lemma or glume *qv*.

Axil: the angle between two structures such as main stem and leaf stalk, hence axillary.

Beak: a narrow projection at the tip of fruits of e.g. cabbage family (*Brassicaceae*) and crane's-bill family (*Geraniaceae*).

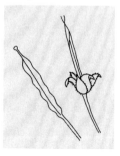

Biennial: a plant that germinates one year, flowers and dies the next *cf* annual and perennial.

Bract: modified leaf usually just below the flower.

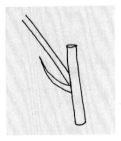

Bracteole: bract-like structure at the base of a compound flower head such as in umbellifers.

Bulb: swollen underground organ made up of modified leaves.

Bulbil: small bulb or tuber above ground usually within leaf axils.

Calcareous: lime-rich or chalky i.e. alkaline rather than acidic.

Calyx: the sepals collectively, usually when they are fused, pl. calyces.

Capitulum: dense head of many single flowers as in the daisy family (*Asteraceae*).

Capsule: a dry, many-seeded fruit that breaks open to release its seeds.

Cleistogamous: of an unopened flower that self-polllinates (see violet).

Corm: swollen underground stem (see rhizome).

Corolla: all the petals of a single flower especially where petals are fused, sometimes referred to as a corolla tube.

Corona: the fused petals or trumpet-shaped part of a daffodil.

Cupule: the fused scales surrounding the nut in the beech family (*Fagaceae*).

Cyme: the curled arrangement of a flower head whereby the first flower is the terminal bud of the main stem and subsequent flowers develop as terminal buds of lateral stems (see comfrey and forget-me-nots).

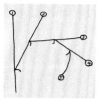

Decumbent: lying flat with tip growing upwards.

Dioecious: having male and female flowers on separate plants.

Disc floret: central part of flowers of daisy family (*Asteraceae*).

Drupe: a succulent fruit holding a single seed with stony coating.

Eusporangiate: having each sporangium developing from more than a single cell, having a wall more than one cell thick and having a large number of spore mother cells.

Filament: stalk of a stamen.

filament

Floret: part of a compound flower such as in the daisy family (*Asteraceae*) or a single flower in grasses (*Poaceae*) or sedges (*Cyperaceae*).

Flush: a boggy area fed by ground water.

Foliate: resembling leaves.

Frond: the leaf of a fern.

Gall: an abnormal outgrowth on plant tissue caused by parasitic insects, fungi or bacteria.

Gametophore: part of a plant-bearing reproductive organ, here referring to a liverwort.

Garden escape: not strictly a wild flower but behaving as such.

Genus: a division of a family of plants including several to many species, pl. genera.

Glabrous: without hairs.

Glaucous: bluish or greyish green in colour.

Glume: in a grass, 1 of 2 outer bracts of the spikelet enclosing the lemma, palea and one or more florets; in a sedge, the bract-like scale in the axil of which lies each individual floret.

Guttation: the release of mineral-rich moisture through the pores of leaves when a plant takes up more water than it can use. Seen in lady's mantle *qv*.

Indusium: small flap or pocket of tissue covering the sporangia in ferns, pl. indusia.

Inflorescence: flowering part of a plant including flowers, branches and bracts.

Insectivorous: feeding on insects (see sundew).

Introduced: a plant that has been brought to this country by man, intentionally or otherwise, rather than by natural means.

Involucre: collectively the sepal-like bracts below the flowers of the daisy family (*Asteraceae*).

Keel: two fused petals at the base of flowers in the pea family (*Fabaceae*). The keel hides the stamens and style.

Labellum: conspicuous lower lip in orchid species.

Lanceolate: long and narrow, like a lance.

Latex: bitter, milky juice found in spurges, dandelions and poppies.

Lemma: one of the scales of a grass flower, see also glume.

Ligule: petal-like structure of ray florets in daisy family (*Asteraceae*); membranous structure in grasses at the base of a leaf blade, important for species identification.

Monoecious: having separate male and female flowers but on the same plant.

Mycorrhizal: a symbiotic association between fungi and the roots of a plant.

Native: a plant that has arrived here by natural means rather than introduced.

Naturalised: a plant that is not native i.e. introduced, but has become established.

Node: where leaves join the stem, sometimes swollen.

Obovate: leaf shape with widest part closer to tip rather than base, see grey willow (*Salix cinerea*).

Ochrea: in dock family, papery sheath at base of the petiole.

Ovary: structure containing the ovules or immature seeds.

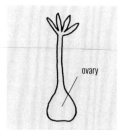

Ovate: a leaf shape with widest part nearer the base.

Palea:: membranous scale within a grass spikelet, see also glume.

Palmate: with finger-like lobes i.e. like the palm of your hand.

Panicle: branched head of flowers.

Pappus: fine hairs in daisy family to aid wind dispersal of seeds – the familiar thistle down and dandelion clocks in *Asteraceae*.

Perennial: of plants that survive for more than two years, more likely to be seen in winter *cf* annual and biennial.

Perianth: outer layers of a flower including sepals and petals, often used when these are very similar and/or fused.

Petal: usually colourful inner part of a flower; not always present.

Petiole: leaf stalk.

Pinna: the primary division of a leaf, pl. pinnae.

Pinnate: of a leaf divided into opposite leaflets along a stalk with a terminal leaflet as in the rose family (*Rosaceae*) and in ferns, hence 1x, 2x, 3x pinnate.

Pinnule: the ultimate division of a divided leaf or frond.

Pistil: female part of a flower comprising stygma, style and ovary.

Pith: the spongy, foam-like substance within the stems of some rushes.

Pollard: to cut off the top of a tree to encourage new growth or a tree so cut. A traditional way of woodland management.

Prickle: sharp, detachable, broad-based appendage derived from the bark, as in roses; does not contain vascular bundles *cf* thorn.

Procumbent: trailing along the ground.

Raceme: an inflorescence where the lowest flowers open first and with a potentially continuously growing apex, hence racemose.

Rachis: the mid-rib of a fern.

Ray floret: outer part of flowers of daisy family (*Asteraceae*).

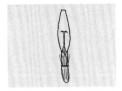

Receptacle: usually swollen area at the top of the flower stalk into which the flower parts are inserted.

Rhizobia: symbiotic bacteria found in the root nodes of the pea family (*Fabaceae*).

Rhizome: horizontal underground stem, hence rhizomatous (see corm).

Runnel: small stream.

Scape: a leafless flower stalk such as in dandelion or primrose.

Sepal: one of the outer segments of a flower enclosing it in bud.

Septa: membranous division along the leaves of some rushes, can be felt as 'joints'.

Sessile: without a stalk.

Sheath: in grasses and sedges, lower part of leaf that encloses the stem.

Silicula: a broad pod of the cabbage family.

Siliqua: a long thin pod of the cabbage family.

Sorus: structure on underside of fern fronds carrying reproductive bodies, pl. sori.

Spadix: cylindrical structure within arum plants at the base of which grow the separate male and female flowers.

Spathe: leaf-like structure surrounding the spadix in arum species.

Species: the basic unit of classification in plants and animals.

Spike: arrangement of flowers in *Carex* species, male spike usually above female.

Spikelet: single unit of an inflorescence in grasses and sedges; in grasses spikelets comprise one or more florets.

Sporangia: bodies that produce spores in ferns and horsetails, sing. sporangium.

Spore: reproductive body of simple plants such as horsetails.

Sport: a plant showing unusual characteristics, different from others of the same species.

Spur: a tubular or pouch-like growth from part of a flower.

Stamen: male part of a flower comprising anther and filament.

Staminode: stamen without an anther, see figwort (*Scrophularia nodosa*).

Standard: erect petal at the top of a flower in the pea family (*Fabaceae*).

Stigma: female part of a flower receptive to the pollen.

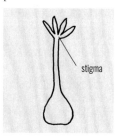

stigma

Stipe: the stalk that bears the frond of a fern.

Strewing herb: a green plant, often aromatic, used for many centuries for scattering on earth floors.

Stipule: leaf-like appendage at base of leaf or petiole, usually in pairs.

Style: part of the female organ of a flower bearing the stigma.

Subspecies: a subdivision of a species.

Succulent: of leaves, thick and fleshy, rich in juice.

Tallow: animal fat.

Tepal: petal-like sepal; name used when petals and sepals indistinguishable from each other.

Thallose: leaf-like structure of a liverwort, pl. thalli.

Thorn: sharp, usually straight, non-detachable appendage derived from branches or stems as in blackthorn; contains vascular tissue *cf* prickle.

Tiller: lateral vegetative shoot arising from the base of a grass stem.

Trifoliate: having three leaflets to each leaf (see trefoils and barren strawberry).

Umbel: umbrella-like compound flower head that may be level or domed at the top.

Umbellifer: member of the carrot family (*Apiaceae*) with flowers in umbels.

Vascular: having to do with the veins or connective tissue of an organ.

Wings: two narrow petals at the sides of flowers in the pea family (*Fabaceae*).

Zygomorphic: having one line of symmetry e.g. violets, orchids and dead-nettles, *cf* actinomorphic.

What to look for throughout the year

This does not include all of the species covered in this book and it can be difficult to pinpoint the appearance of some species especially following a hard winter or a particularly early warm spell but the following provides a guide of what to look for when and what you *might* find in flower at any particular month in the year. It should be remembered, however, that some species, such as roses, sedges and umbellifers, can be more easily identified in fruit rather than flower.

January
Winter heliotrope, groundsel, sticky buds of horse-chestnut and the black tips of ash trees.

February
Lesser celandine, barren strawberry, coltsfoot and snowdrops.

March
Hazel catkins, wood anemone, round-leaved crowfoot, white dead-nettle and marsh marigolds.

April
Garlic mustard, greater stitchwort, sweet cicely, greater celandine, primrose, dog violet, wild daffodil and blackthorn.

May
Large bittercress, dame's violet, wood sorrel, red campion, eyebright, pignut, tormentil, crosswort, bush vetch, pink purslane, milkwort, speedwells, bluebells, wild arum, broom, hawthorn, elder, meadow foxtail, horsetails, glaucous sedge, soft brome and sweet vernal grass.

June
Bedstraws, chickweed-wintergreen, feverfew, bird's foot trefoil, slender St John's wort, yellow rattle, poppy, bitter vetchling, ragged robin, roses, great wood-rush, cottongrasses, mat-grass and Yorkshire fog.

July
Yarrow, valerian, hedge parsley, pale lady's mantle, betony, hedge woundwort, honeysuckle, bog asphodel and quaking grass.

August
Sneezewort, wild angelica, cow-wheat, meadow crane's-bill, wood burdock, spear thistle, scabious, brooklime, several rushes and sedges.

September
Many plants now in fruit but meadowsweet, herb bennet and field scabious can still be found in flower.

October

Round-leaved water-crowfoot still to be found as well as clovers, greater celandine and white dead-nettle and of course many of the trees will be in their splendid autumn colours.

November

Shepherd's purse can still be found as well as chickweed and mouse-ear.

December

Daisies and yarrow can still be found in flower as well as viburnum.

Where to find wild flowers in Westerdale

The following is not an exhaustive list as many wild plants are found along most of the lanes and some are very common but this is to help in the location of some of the more interesting species when they are in season.

From the village walking north past Huntersty bridge look for hart's tongue, wild ramsons, meadow crane's-bill, aspen, milkwort, eyebright, yellow rattle, crab apple and field horsetail.

From the village walking south and then west to Wood End look for turkey oak, water crowfoot, milkwort, hedge woundwort and soft rush.

From the village walking east towards Castleton look for hazel, common valerian, bitter vetchling, bay willow, goat willow, fairy flax and round-leaved mint.

From the village walking east towards Westerdaleside look for scaly male fern, common figwort, cat's-ear, autumn hawkbit, brooklime, pignut and Sherard's rose.

From the village walking west towards Westerdale Hall and Grange Farm look for wild arum, snowdrops, larch, sycamore, winter heliotrope, pale lady's mantle, wild daffodils and bluebells.

At Hob Hole look for musk and lemon-scented fern.

References

For plant identification the following volumes have been consulted:

Anstey, Faith, *Start to Identify Sedges and Rushes*. Perth: printed by Farquhar & Son Ltd, published by Wildflower Study, 2019.[1]

Blamey, Marjorie & Fitter, Richard & Alistair, *Wild Flowers of Britain and Ireland*. London: Bloomsbury Publishing, second edition 2013.

Cope, Tom & Gray, Alan, *Grasses of the British Isles*. BSBI handbook No. 13. London: Botanical Society of the British Isles 2009.

Grey-Wilson, Christopher & Blamey, Marjorie, *The Illustrated Flora of Britain and Northern Europe*. London: Hodder and Stoughton, 1989.

Harding, Patrick & Tomblin, Gill, *How to Identify Trees*. London: HarperCollins Publishers Ltd, 1998.

Jermy, A C, Simpson, D A, Foley, M J Y & Porter, M S, *Sedges of the British Isles* BSBI handbook No. 1, Edition 3. London, Botanical Society of the British Isles 2016.

Johnson, Owen & More, David, *Collins Tree Guide*. London: HarperCollins Publishers Ltd, 2004.

Keble-Martin, W, *The New Concise British Flora*. London, Bloomsbury Books, 1982, first published 1965.

Mabey, Richard, *Flora Britannica: the definitive new guide to wild flowers, plants and trees*. London: Sinclair-Stevenson, Reed International Books Ltd, 1996.

Phillips, Roger, *Grasses, Ferns, Mosses & Lichens of Great Britain and Ireland*. London: Pan Books Ltd, 1980.

Phillips, Roger, *Wild Flowers of Britain*. London: Pan Books Ltd, 1977.

Rose, Francis, *Grasses, Sedges, Rushes and Ferns*. London: Penguin Books, 1989.

Rose, Francis, *The Wild Flower Key*. Revised and updated by Clare O'Reilly. London: Penguin Books, 2006. (First published by Frederick Warne, 1981.)

Ross-Craig, Stella, *Drawings of British Plants*. Parts I – XXXI. London: G Bell & Sons Ltd, 1951-1973.

Stace, Clive, *New Flora of the British Isles*. Cambridge: Cambridge University Press, third edition 2010, reprinted 2014.[2]

Streeter, David, *Collins Flower Guide*. London: HarperCollins Publishers Ltd, 2010.

Sykes, Nan, *Picture Guide to the Wild Flowers of North East Yorkshire*. Helmsley: North York Moors National Park Authority, 2008.

For further information please see the website of the BSBI and the Facebook page of the North East Yorkshire Botany Group.

---

1. Highly recommended for beginners.
2. Not for the faint-hearted, but this is the authoritative work on any plant likely to be found in the British Isles.

For folklore, medicinal and other uses of plants the following volumes have been consulted:

Bremness, Lesley, *The Complete Book of Herbs: a practical guide to growing and using herbs*. London: Dorling Kindersley in association with the National Trust, 1990.

Browning, Gareth H, *The Naming of Wild-Flowers*. London: Williams and Norgate Ltd, 1952.

Campbell-Culver, Maggie, *The Origin of Plants: the people and plants that have shaped Britain's Garden History since the year 1000*. London: Hodder Headline, 2001.

Coombes, Allen J, *The Collingridge Dictionary of Plant Names*. London: Collingridge Books, 1990.

Genders, Roy, *The Scented Wild Flowers of Britain*. London: Collins, 1971.

Grieve, Mrs M, *A Modern Herbal*. Harmondsworth: Penguin Books Ltd, 1978.

Grigson, Geoffrey, *A Dictionary of English Plant Names*. London: Alan Lane, 1974.

Grigson, Geoffrey, *The Englishman's Flora*. Oxford: Helicon Publishing Ltd, 1975.

Hall, Charles A., *A Pocket-Book of British Wild Flowers*. London: A & C Black, 1944.

Hyde, Molly, *Hedgerow Plants*. Aylesbury: Shire Publications Ltd, 1976.

Pokorný Jaromír, *A Colour Guide to Familiar Trees: Leaves, Bark and Fruit*. London: Octopus Books Ltd, 1977. (First published in Prague in 1973, translated by Olga Kuthanová.)

Richardson, Rosamond, *Britain's Wild Flowers: a treasury of traditions, superstitions, remedies and literature*. London, National Trust Books, 2017.

Sterndale-Bennett, Jane, *Plant Names Explained*. Winchester: OutHouse Publishing for David & Charles, 2005.

Westell, Percival W, *Wild Flowers of the Wood*. London: T Werner Laurie (date unrecorded, early twentieth century).

Woodward, Marcus (Ed.), *Gerard's Herbal: the history of plants*. London: Studio Editions Ltd, 1994.

Wordsworth Reference, *Culpeper's Complete Herbal: A book of natural remedies for ancient ills*. Ware: Wordsworth Editions Ltd, 1995.

Index of botanical names

Index of common names

Botanical update

As we went to press, the fourth edition of Stace's *Flora of the British Isles* was published. This is considered to be the definitive authority on plant nomenclature and includes several changes to plant names as a result of recent DNA analysis and/or the discovery of an earlier name. The relevant scientific names of crack willow and of the roses have been amended for this book but these additional changes should be noted:

Anagallis tenella (bog pimpernel) is now *Lysimachia tenella*

Anthemis tinctoria (yellow chamomile) is now *Cota tinctoria*

Deschampsia flexuosa (wavy hair-grass) is now *Avenella flexuosa*

Chamerion angustifolium (rosebay willowherb) is now *Chamaenerion angustifolium*

Mecanopsis cambrica (Welsh poppy) is now *Papaver cambricum*

Papaver orientale (Oriental poppy) is now *Papaver setiferum*

Petasites fragrans (winter heliotrope) is now *Petasites pyrenaicus*

Polygonum arenastrum (equal-leaved knotgrass) is now *Polygonum depressum*

Senecio jacobaea (common ragwort) is now *Jacobaea vulgaris*

Please note that crack willow is now designated *Salix x fragilis* rather than *Salix fragilis* as this has been shown to be a hybrid between white willow (*S. alba*) and eastern crack willow (*S. euxina*).

For readers' interest – in this fourth edition, Stace records that English elm is 'apparently a Roman introduction.'

Three-nerved sandwort (*Moehringia trinervia*) has recently been found in Westerdale.

For your own botanical notes…